Outward Dreams

Outward Dreams
Black Inventors and Their Inventions

Jim Haskins

Walker and Company
New York

First published in the United States of America in 1991
by Walker Publishing Company, Inc.

Published simultaneously in Canada by Thomas Allen & Son
Canada, Limited, Markham, Ontario

Library of Congress Cataloging-in-Publication Data

Haskins, James, date.
Outward dreams : Black inventors and their inventions / Jim
Haskins.
p.   cm.
Includes bibliographical references and index.
Summary: Discusses black inventors and their contributions,
including Benjamin Bradley, Madam Walker, and George Washington
Carver.
ISBN 0-8027-6993-4. — ISBN 0-8027-6994-2 (reinf.)
1. Afro-American inventors—United States—Biography—Juvenile
literature.   [1. Inventors. 2. Afro-Americans—Biography.]
I. Title.
T39.H37   1991
609.2′2—dc20
[B]
[920]   90-12973
CIP
AC

Printed in the United States of America

2   4   6   8   10   9   7   5   3   1

to

Margaret Emily

acknowledgments

I am grateful to Anne Jordan, Ann Kalkhoff, and Kathy Benson for their help. For assistance in obtaining photographs, I would also like to thank Mrs. Winifred L. Norman, niece of Lewis H. Latimer, and Portia P. James, curator of the exhibition "The Real McCoy: African-American Invention and Innovation, 1619–1930" at the Smithsonian Institution.

contents

chapter
1

INGENUITY,
PATENTS,
AND PATIENCE

*L*ong before recorded history, mankind had
sought to ease the burden of everyday life by
finding ways to make a task less tiresome and
onerous. In all likelihood the first "inventions" by early
man were such basics as fire, the wheel, and cooking,
things that not only made life less harsh but also led to
further innovation and discovery. The early "inventors"
set out to change the world, as inventors have continued to do ever since. The same curiosity that spurred a
"cave inventor" to throw his meat on a burning tree has
generated the technological marvels that emerge—
almost every second it seems—today. In 1989, there
were about 152,000 patent applications filed in the
United States, and that number will only increase each
year thereafter. An inventor seeks not only to better his

or her world. Invention is a means of gaining recognition or financial reward for the long, often solitary hours of labor, hence the creation of the patent.

A patent is granted by the government and permits an inventor to have a temporary monopoly over his or her invention. Inventors are given recognition for their creations through the issuance of a patent and are given the exclusive right to manufacture, sell, or use the product of their ingenuity; no one else may do so without the permission of the holder of the patent.

Because of so-called "American ingenuity," and the number of inventions by Americans, we tend to think that the idea of granting a patent originated here in the United States, but patents were in existence even before Columbus set foot in the New World. A Florentine received a patent in 1421, and Venice enacted a patent law in 1474. In the mid-sixteenth century, England began to grant patents for inventions. During the reign of James I, 1603–1625, all royal monopolies were outlawed except patents given specifically to inventors of "newe Manufactures." Until the end of the American Revolution, most colonies in America followed the patent laws of England. Some, however, rather than granting patents, rewarded inventors for their inventions in money or land—what James Madison called "premiums and provisions." It was not until 1790 that a uniform Act was passed by the new United States government for the purpose of granting patents to American inventors.

The Act of 1790 established a patent board made up of the Secretaries of State and War and the Attorney

General. Their job was "to grant patents for any useful art, manufacture, engine, machine, or device as they should deem sufficiently useful and important." This act was soon superseded by a new patent law in 1793 due to the absurdity of having members of the president's cabinet serving as processors of patent applications.

Under the new patent law of 1793, applications were not examined. One could obtain a patent merely by paying $30.00 and swearing that one was the "true inventor." This new patent law led to a great deal of abuse. People patented ideas and processes that had been in use for years or even centuries. Many prominent inventors, Eli Whitney among them, protested this law and lobbied for a reinstatement of the examination process whereby applications were examined with an eye to "prior art"—whether the invention is already in existence or not—and to establish the originality and newness of the device or idea. In 1836 the protestors were successful, the examination system was reinstated, and the Patent Office was established, marking the beginning of the modern patent process in the United States.

When a patent application is received by the U.S. Patent Office, not only is it examined with a view to prior art, but also to the usefulness and workability of the invention. When the Patent Office considers usefulness, however, it is following the definition of *useful* that was established by the Supreme Court in 1817. In 1817, Associate Justice Joseph Story ruled in a case that was brought before the Court that "useful," when referring to the invention process, meant *not* "frivolous or injurious to the well-being, good policy, or sound morals of society." From this perspective, an invention may be useful, in the sense of not being harmful, and, at the same time, useless, as it may be of little benefit to anyone.

The Patent Office also considers whether a particular invention works or not, although, within this framework, it has been determined that the discovery of a natural law cannot be patented. A natural law, such as gravity, may "work" but belongs to everyone.

The issuance of a patent is intended to reward the inventor and to encourage more and better inventions. In the United States this practice has both succeeded and failed. Inventions have led to further and better inventions, but the inventor has not always received his or her just reward or the recognition either may deserve. This is particularly true of black inventors in the United States.

Under the patent laws of 1793 and 1836, black slaves and freedmen alike were permitted to patent their inventions. Slaves, however, frequently lost their inventions to their masters who claimed the inventions as their own and patented them under their own names. Black freedmen fared slightly better. In 1821 Thomas L. Jennings became the first black person known to patent an invention when he was issued a patent for a dry-cleaning process. Jennings used the money generated by his patent and by his dry-cleaning and tailoring business in New York City as so many

black freedmen did at this time: to support the abolitionist cause.

Another early black inventor did not prosper as
greatly from his invention. In 1854, Henry Sigler, a
free black of Galveston, Texas, patented an improved
fishhook. Unfortunately, he later sold his patent for a
mere $625.

In 1857, a slaveowner, Oscar J. E. Stuart, applied
for a patent for a "double cotton scraper" that had
been invented by his slave, Ned. Stuart's rationale for
patenting Ned's invention in his own name was that
"the master is the owner of the fruits of the labor of the
slave both intellectual and manual." The government
denied Stuart's application, but the case called to its
attention the entire issue of permitting slaves to patent
their inventions when Stuart then tried to patent the
invention in Ned's name. The government also denied
Ned's right to a patent because he was a slave and, in
1858, the United States Attorney General put a stop to
the patenting of any inventions by slaves. He ruled that
slaves were not citizens and therefore could not be
granted patents. In time, all black people, both slave
and free, were affected by this ruling. Ironically, in
1861, the Confederate States of America, which was
made up of those states that supported the institution
of slavery, passed a law granting patents to slaves.

It was not until after the Civil War that the United
States once again consented to recognize black ingenu-
ity and invention. The passage of the Thirteenth and
Fourteenth Amendments made blacks citizens of the

United States. By 1870 there were hundreds of applications by blacks on file at the Patent Office for inventions that were to affect the everyday lives of people, black and white, around the world.

From the earliest years of the United States, not only were many blacks forced to endure the shackles of slavery, but they were also forced to contend with the white man's attitude that they were inferior and lacking in intelligence and ingenuity. In conquering the wilderness of the New World, blacks had brought with them from Africa and other places a vast array of knowledge that resulted in the invention of everything from tools for simple household use to intricate and complex machinery. The names of many of these early inventors have been lost in time, but one of them is still remembered not only for his skill in invention but also for his genius in mathematics. Benjamin Banneker (1731–1806) not only displayed ingenuity in his mathematical computations but demonstrated to all that the black man was not inferior nor lacking in intelligence.

chapter
2

*"A VERY
RESPECTABLE
MATHEMATICIAN"*

By the time of his death in 1806, Benjamin Banneker, a free-born Negro from Baltimore County, Maryland, had earned the respect of presidents and was lauded as a mathematical genius. He had fulfilled, many times over, all the hopes both his parents and his grandmother had had for him when he was born on the small Maryland farm known as Bannaky Springs in 1731. And those hopes had been high.

Molly Walsh, Benjamin's grandmother, was a white English woman who had come to America as an indentured servant in 1685. Under the terms of her indentureship she was obligated to work seven years to earn her freedom. In 1692, when Molly was twenty-two

years old, she was finally free to do as she wished in the
new land of America.

Molly was a hard worker with a great deal of independence and determination. In 1692, the colony of
Maryland was largely undeveloped, and there was
so much free land that anyone could claim for himself
all the land he could farm and develop. Molly claimed
and settled on a one-hundred-and-fifty-acre farm site,
determined to make a home and a living from this
land. Although she was young and strong, Molly real-
ized that she would need help cultivating her land and
so she purchased two male slaves, one named Martin,
the other a man of African origin named Bannaky.

Working side by side, clearing the land and planting crops, Molly quickly earned the respect of her two
slaves and, in turn, came to respect them. Before long,
Molly gave them both their freedom and shortly after-
ward accepted the proposal of marriage from Bannaky.
As Bannaky had no last name, Molly created a last
name, Banneker, from his name.

Marriage between white, indentured servants and
black slaves was not uncommon in the colonies at that
time although it was frowned upon. Indeed, an act
passed in 1715 strictly forbade ministers or magistrates
from marrying any white person to "any Negro or
Mulatto slave." But Molly and Bannaky lived some
distance from any large city or town and both they and
the local authorities were unaware of the Act of 1715.
Molly and Bannaky were married and began happily
raising four children.

Molly and Bannaky's eldest daughter was a pretty

girl named Mary. When Mary was about sixteen years old she met and fell in love with a handsome slave named Robert who was owned by the master of a nearby plantation. When Mary told Molly about Robert, Molly bought and freed him and the two young people were married. As he had no last name of his own, being a slave, Robert adopted Mary's last name and became Robert Banneker. Robert and Mary settled with Molly on the land at Bannaky Springs and began raising their own family; in 1731 their son, Benjamin, was born.

Molly taught young Benjamin and his sisters to read, write, and count. Benjamin, even at an early age, showed his love for numbers and for "figuring things out." When he was older, Benjamin was sent to a Quaker "pay" school near his home. The Quakers had long spoken out against slavery and discrimination because of color, and the master at Benjamin's school insisted on accepting all children, black or white, into his school.

Benjamin's interest in mathematics and mechanics grew under the tutelage of the Quaker schoolmaster, and, even after he had completed the limited courses offered by the school, he continued to study and learn on his own. He was fascinated by how things were put together, and soon came to the attention of George Ellicott, a Quaker neighbor whose flour mills were the largest industry in the region. Ellicott loaned young Benjamin books to read and encouraged him in his pursuit of knowledge. Later, under Ellicott's influence, Benjamin also developed an enthusiasm for astronomy.

What had drawn Ellicott's attention to Benjamin was a clock. At the age of twenty-four, in 1754, Benjamin Banneker had demonstrated his skill and knowledge of mechanical things by building a clock. Constructed of wood, the clock not only told the time of day, but also struck the hour. Banneker's clock is believed to be the first clock made in the United States and, so good a craftsman was Banneker, it kept correct time all his life.

During the day, Benjamin devoted himself to farming the family land; only at night did he have the time to devote to his reading and studies. As he grew older, he gave up farming, selling part of the land and leasing the rest to other farmers. Neighbors thought him strange and lazy because he slept all day and, wrapped in a cloak, roamed the land at night. What they didn't know was that Benjamin was busy calculating the movement of the stars, his ambition being to publish the most accurate almanac yet seen. Although his neighbors thought him a bit crazy, his name was soon to be known to the highest leaders of the United States and was to be mentioned with great respect.

Following the Revolutionary War, George Washington set up a commission to design a capital city for the new United States. Andrew Ellicott, the son of George Ellicott, and Benjamin Banneker's longtime friend, was chosen as a planner by the commission. He felt that Banneker would be invaluable to such a project and so brought Benjamin's name to the attention of Washington. Washington and James McHenry, the senator from Maryland, convinced the commission to appoint Benja-

In 1754, at the age of twenty-four, Benjamin Banneker built what is believed to be the first clock made in the United States. (Moorland-Spingarn Research Center, Howard University)

min Banneker and Andrew Ellicott as surveyors and mathematicians in the planning of Washington, D.C. "I accepted this honor with great pride," Banneker said, "not for myself but for my race." Banneker had long been concerned by the idea, promoted by many whites, that blacks were inferior. He accepted the appointment because he wished to prove that the black man was *not* the intellectual inferior of the white man. With his acceptance, Benjamin Banneker became the first black man to receive a presidential appointment.

When Ellicott and Banneker set to work, a Frenchman, Pierre Charles L'Enfant, was to be the chief architect and head the project. The *Georgetown Weekly Ledger* wrote of the arrival of Ellicott and L'Enfant and noted they were accompanied by "Benjamin Banneker, an Ethiopian."

The three men selected a site on the Potomac River for the new capital and set about surveying and planning. However, after laying out the city, L'Enfant resigned as a result of an argument with Federal officials. Angry, he left America, taking all the plans with him. The officials were in a quandary as to how the city was to be completed—the plans were gone! Fortunately, Benjamin Banneker and his incredible memory came to their rescue. While working with Ellicott and L'Enfant, he had memorized all the plans and was able to draw them from memory. The Commission then ordered that "as soon as performable, Benjamin Banneker would deliver to the Secretary of State, the Honorable Thomas Jefferson, a complete set of plans for the city of Washington and the District of Columbia."

Because of Benjamin Banneker, the city we know today as the capital city of the United States was built.

Before, during and after Banneker's work for the Commission, he continued to pursue his studies, particularly those involving astronomy. In 1792, the fruit of his labors was publicly produced. Although he had handwritten an almanac in 1791, it was not until 1792 that he was able to find a publisher for *Benjamin Banneker's Pennsylvania, Delaware, Virginia, and Maryland Almanack and Ephemeris.*

An almanac is a table or a calendar of days and months with the astronomical information for each noted. The phases of the moon are indicated and the times of high and low tides, the best planting times, and other useful information. Banneker's almanac for 1792 also included amusing stories and an article about Banneker himself by James McHenry. In it McHenry noted that the almanac was "fresh proof that the powers of the mind are [not connected to] the color of the skin."

This idea, voiced by McHenry, together with the issue of slavery, were of great concern to Banneker. Earlier, hoping to find support both for his almanac and for his belief that blacks were not inferior, Benjamin had sent a handwritten copy of his almanac for 1791 to Thomas Jefferson, who was then Secretary of State. In his letter to Jefferson, Benjamin Banneker reminded him of:

> *that time in which the arms and tyranny of the British Crown were exerted with every powerful*

13

The cover of Benjamin Banneker's almanac, published in 1795. (Moorland-Spingarn Research Center, Howard University)

*effort, in order to reduce you to a state of servi-
tude. Look back, I entreat you, to the variety
of dangers to which every human aid appeared
unavailable, and in which even hope and forti-
tude wore the aspect of inability to the conflict,
and you cannot but be led to a serious and grateful sense of your miraculous and providential
preservation.*

*You cannot but acknowledge that the present
freedom and tranquility which you enjoy you have
mercifully received, and that it is the peculiar
blessing of Heaven.*

*This, sir, was a time in which you clearly
saw into the injustice of slavery and in which you
had just apprehensions of the horrors of its condition; it was now, sir, that your abhorrence thereof
was so excited that you publicly held forth this
true and invaluable doctrine, which is worthy to
be recorded and remembered in all succeeding
ages:*

*"We hold these truths to be self-evident, that
all men are created equal, and that they are
endowed by their Creator with certain inalienable
rights, that amongst these are life, liberty and the
pursuit of happiness."*

*Here, sir, was a time in which your tender
feelings for yours engaged you thus to declare;
you were then impressed with a proper idea of the
just valuation of liberty, and the free possession of
those blessings to which you were entitled by
nature, but sir, how pitiable it is to reflect, that
although you were so fully convinced of the
benevolence of the Father of Mankind, and of His
equal and impartial distribution of those rights
and privileges which He had conferred upon*

15

them, that you should, at the same time, counter-
act His mercies, in detaining by fraud and vio-
lence so numerous a part of my brethren, under
groaning captivity and oppression; that you
should, at the same time, be found guilty of that
most criminal act, which you professedly detested
in others with respect to yourselves. . . .

And now, sir, although my sympathy and
affection for my brethren hath caused my enlarge-
ment thus far, I ardently hope that your candor
and generosity will plead with you in my behalf,
when I make known to you that it was not origi-
nally my design, but having taken up my pen
in order to direct to you, as a present a copy of an
almanac which I have calculated for the ensuing
year, I was unexpectedly led thereto.

Jefferson was greatly impressed by the almanac
and sympathetic to Banneker's views. As he states in a
letter to Benjamin in 1791,

No body wishes more than I do to see such
proofs as you exhibit, that nature has given our
black brethren, talents equal to those of the other
colors of men, and that the appearance of a want
of them is owing merely to the degraded condition
of their existence, both in Africa and Ameri-
ca. . . . I have taken the liberty of sending your
Almanac to Monsieur de Condorcet, Secretary of
the Academy of Sciences at Paris, and member of
the Philanthropic Society, because I considered it
as a document to which your whole color had a
right for their justification against the doubts
which have been entertained of them.

In his letter to Monsieur de Condorcet, Jefferson praised Banneker's almanac, adding,

> *I have seen very elegant solutions of geometrical problems by him. Add to this that he is a very worthy and respectable member of society.*

Benjamin Banneker saw his almanac not only as a useful tool for predicting the weather and the seasons, but as a way to help his oppressed race. Because blacks were enslaved, others thought of them as slow-witted. Here was proof that this was not true, proof confirmed by one of the greatest living white leaders, Thomas Jefferson himself.

Banneker continued to compose a new almanac for each of the following years. The 1795 almanac had a portrait of Benjamin wearing his usual simple Quaker clothing. It proved so popular that copies were made by at least nine different printers. Readers of this almanac came to realize that his almanac was the most accurate of those available at that time and they enjoyed the stories and riddles and other information he included. In 1802, however, Banneker stopped writing his almanac. He did not give a reason for abandoning the work, but it is likely that, at the age of seventy-one, he wished to rest and devote himself to his other interests.

On October 25, 1806, a Sunday, Benjamin Banneker took a last walk through the woods at Bannaky Springs. Tired, on his return Benjamin lay down to rest and peacefully died in his sleep. The announcement of his death in the *Federal Gazette* and *Baltimore Daily Advertiser* of October 28, 1806, read:

> *On Sunday, the 25th instant, departed this life,*
> *near his residence in Baltimore County, Mr.*
> *Benjamin Banneker, a black man, immediate*
> *descendant of an African father. He was known*
> *in this neighborhood for his quiet and peaceful*
> *demeanor and among scientific men, as an*
> *astronomer and mathematician.*

On the day of Banneker's funeral, his cabin burned to the ground. It was the cabin in which he had been born and raised, in which he had studied and learned so much, giving that learning to others through his writings and his almanac. In it were not only his almanacs and correspondence, but the wooden clock he had made so many years before that still kept perfect time. Although Benjamin Banneker's possessions were gone, his memory remains and has served as an inspiration not only to other, later black scientists and inventors, but also to those who, like Banneker, worked for equality and freedom for blacks. In all ways, he can be compared to the watchmaker in the poem, *Epitaph for a Watch-Maker,* that appeared in his almanac for 1797:

> *Integrity was the main spring*
> *And prudence was the regulator*
> *Of all the actions of his life.*
> *Humane, generous and liberal*
> *His hand never stopped*
> *Till he had relieved distress*

chapter 3

UNREWARDED DREAMS

W hile Benjamin Banneker was inventing elegant mathematical formulas to calculate the weather and various astronomical events, other black inventors were having a more material impact on society with their inventions, although only a few of them were able to receive patents; many were refused the recognition and rewards they deserved because they were slaves.

Before the Civil War the majority of blacks in the United States were slaves and seven out of eight slaves worked on plantations, mainly in the Deep South. Many of the inventions and devices they created were designed to ease the hardship of their condition and make the backbreaking work they did a bit easier. One slave, for example, named Joe Anderson, helped Cyrus

McCormick invent his famous reaper, although in most histories Anderson is not credited for the help he gave McCormick. Another, Benjamin Montgomery, a slave owned by Jefferson Davis, invented, in the late 1850's, a boat propellor that made the propelling and steering of boats less arduous.

Free blacks, similarly, looked to ease the burden of their labor and many of these are remembered, unlike the slave inventors whose names have been forgotten for the most part. Patent Office records, for example, show that "a colored man," Henry Blair, was granted patents for a seedplanter for corn and a seedplanter for cotton in 1834. Both inventions sped up the planting process and reduced the amount of hand labor needed to sow crops.

In the 1840's another black inventor, Lewis Temple, came up with a device that revolutionized the whaling industry. Temple was a blacksmith in New Bedford, Massachusetts, although he had been born in Richmond, Virginia, in 1800. At that time, New Bedford was a bustling New England sea town and the center for the whaling industry. One of Temple's common jobs was to forge harpoons for the whalers and, through this work, Temple learned that whales would often escape after being harpooned. In 1848 he invented a toggle-harpoon which has been called the most important invention in the history of whaling. Temple's harpoon made it more difficult for the whales, once harpooned, to escape. It soon became the standard harpoon used in the whaling industry and it revolutionized whaling. Temple himself, unfortunately, didn't share in the increased wealth generated by his invention; he had never patented it. In 1854 he died a poor man.

Unlike Temple, James Forten, a free black of Philadelphia, profited from his invention, and went on to use his wealth for the abolitionist cause. Born in 1766, Forten attended a Quaker school as a boy. After his schooling was finished, he was apprenticed to a sailmaker but his apprenticeship was interrupted when the Revolution broke out. Forten served as a powder boy in the Navy during the American Revolution, and, after the war, with his Naval background and sailmaking experience, he was able to find a good job in a sail factory. Forten advanced quickly in his job and in his spare time began championing the cause of abolition, speaking out against slavery and for the right of black people to live freely in America.

Sometime after 1800, Forten invented a device that aided in the control of sails on ships. His invention made him one of the wealthiest men in America; in all, it is estimated he earned $100,000 from his invention, an enormous amount of money at that time. His wealth enabled him to build his own sail factory which employed fifty black and white workers, and also to support the causes to which he was dedicated. He gave a considerable sum of money to William Lloyd Garrison's abolitionist newspaper, *The Liberator,* and helped solicit many of its 1700 black subscribers. A strong supporter of the United States government, he also helped to

James Forten. (The Historical Society of Pennsylvania)

recruit black soldiers during the War of 1812, and aided in running an Underground Railroad, helping slaves escape to freedom.

The cause of abolition was the one that Forten felt the most strongly about, however, and one to which he devoted most of his attention and money. As he questioned in one of the early issues of *The Liberator,*

> *Has the God who made the white man and the black left any record declaring us a different species? Are we not sustained by the same power, supported by the same food, hurt by the same wounds, wounded by the same wrongs, pleased with the same delights, and propagated by the same means? And should we not then enjoy the same liberty, and be protected by the same laws?*

Unfortunately, James Forten died in 1842, twenty years before the fruits of his abolitionist efforts would blossom. He left behind, however, a standard of excellence in his eloquence, industry, and generosity that many have emulated since, and an invention that modernized the sailing industry in many ways.

Just as Forten's invention helped further the cause of freedom, the inventiveness of another man led to freedom itself. Benjamin Bradley was born a slave around 1830, but his natural mechanical skills so astounded others that they helped to buy him his freedom. Bradley himself contributed money toward his own freedom and was later able to pay back all those who had helped him. A letter to one of those contributors explains Bradley's background.

Bradley was owned by a master in Annapolis, Maryland. Eight years ago he was employed in a printing office there. He was then about sixteen, and showed great mechanical skill and ingenuity. With a piece of gun-barrel, some pewter, a couple of pieces of round steel, and some materials, he constructed a working model of a steam engine.

His master soon afterwards got him the place of a helper in the department of Natural and Experimental Philosophy at the Naval Academy at Annapolis. He sold his first steam engine to a Midshipman. With the proceeds, and what money he could lay up (his master allowing him five dollars a month out of his wages), he built an engine large enough to drive the first cutter of a sloop-of-war at the rate of sixteen knots an hour. . . .

Professor Hopkins, of the Academy, says that he sets up the experiments for the lecture-room very handsomely. Being shown once how to line up the parabolic mirrors for concentrating heat, he always succeeds afterwards. So with chemical experiments. He makes all the gasses, and works with them, showing the Drummond lights, &c. Professor Hopkins remarks of him that "he looks for the law *by which things act."*

He has been taught to read and write, mainly by the Professor's children; has made very good progress in arithmetic, and will soon take hold of algebra and geometry.

Benjamin Bradley learned the principles and mathematics that lay behind the steam engines he built only *after* he had built them. Fortunately his skill and genius did not go unrecognized or unrewarded. Although he was unable to patent his work under United States law, which forbade a slave from patenting his invention, through the efforts of his friends he was remembered and was rewarded for his ability with his freedom.

Another pre–Civil War inventor who, because of the laws, could not patent his invention, was Henry Boyd (1802–1886). Boyd was a furniture maker in Cincinnati, Ohio, when he thought up the "Boyd Bedstead," an improved wooden bedframe. His bedframe proved to be very popular with his customers and Boyd made quite a bit of money from it. He enlisted the aid of a white cabinetmaker who patented it and thus protected the rights to the design.

The inventions of Blair, Boyd, Temple, Forten, and Bradley were the natural extensions of their work and interests. These were only a few of the men and women who, before the Civil War, followed the paths of inventors to improve their products or their lives in general. Because blacks were forbidden patents after 1858 until 1870, there are few records of the many other inventors who may have existed at that time.

The Civil War turned brother against brother and split the nation in two. Even before the war itself, southerners were becoming increasingly defensive about their "peculiar institution," slavery. With the passage of the Fugitive Slave Act in 1850, controls on blacks, both slave and free, became more harsh; what little freedom they did have was sharply curtailed. One

inventor who felt the restrictions keenly, ironically
also contributed to the industry of the South: Norbert
Rillieux, who revolutionized the sugar refining
industry.

chapter
4

INGENUITY

AND

CONFLICT

*I*n the late 1840's, Dr. Charles Browne, sugar chemist of the U.S. Department of Agriculture, wrote,

> *Rillieux's invention is the greatest in the history of*
> *American chemical engineering, and I know of*
> *no other invention that has brought so great a*
> *saving to all branches of chemical engineering.*

What Browne was referring to was a revolutionary new system developed by Norbert Rillieux for processing sugar, a system that was eventually adapted for other refining processes as well.

Norbert Rillieux (1806–1894) was born in the rambunctious, bustling city of New Orleans. His father was master of a plantation on which his mother was a

slave. Even at an early age Rillieux displayed an un-
usual intelligence and his father fostered it, sending
him to Paris to be educated, as at that time schools in
New Orleans which would have been suitable for Rillieux's ability refused to admit black students. Young
Rillieux grew up in Paris and after his schooling was
completed, at the age of twenty-four, became a teacher
at L'Ecole Centrale in Paris where he taught applied
mechanics. During this time Rillieux wrote a number
of scientific papers on the steam engine and steam
economy, papers that illustrated his fascination with
doing things better, doing things faster.

America seemed to be where things were happen-
ing, however, and where technology seemed to be
nurtured, so Rillieux eventually returned to his native
New Orleans, where he hoped to put some of his ideas
into practice. He went to work as an engineer in the
sugar refining industry, one of the largest industries in
New Orleans at that time. As he had with steam engines, he started analyzing the sugar refining process,
studying ways to make it more efficient.

Until the 1840's, the refining of sugar cane juice
into granular sugar was done by a long, laborious and
primitive method known as the "Jamaica Train." This
method consisted of two men (usually slaves) pouring
boiling sugar back and forth from one huge caldron to
another until it congealed into large, brown lumps.
The process not only took a long time but was expensive and hazardous. Attempts had been made by other
scientists, notably Howard and DeGrand, to simplify
this sugar refining process by using vacuum pans and

condensing coils, but these did not work as the scientists had envisioned. In 1843, however, Rillieux, who was chief engineer by then, obtained his first patent for a vacuum evaporation system. The system enclosed the condensing coils in a vacuum chamber and used the vapor from this first chamber to evaporate the juice in a second chamber under higher vacuum.

Rillieux's employers were astounded. His system cut production costs enormously, resulted in a better quality of sugar, and made that sugar easily affordable. His system was quickly adopted by his own refinery. Soon all the sugar refineries in the United States were using Rillieux's process and it was spreading to other countries.

Norbert Rillieux rapidly became one of the wealthiest and most important men in Louisiana because of his sugar refining system. He was admired for his genius and money by some; others, however, saw his success as a threat. They saw only the color of his skin and were eager to deny him, as they denied all blacks, the same rights as those extended to whites.

The 1850's were a time of tension for the South. The 1850 Fugitive Slave Act passed by the United States government was designed to discourage anyone from helping a runaway slave. But, particularly in the North, it had an effect opposite to that intended. Abolitionists saw the Act as a challenge and the Underground Railroad assumed a strength it had not possessed before. Northern abolitionists posted notices describing slave catchers and harassed white southerners who traveled north. In the South, all this abolitionist activity only

intensified fear of slave rebellions and fear of slaves
escaping to freedom. In the border states between the
North and South, clashes broke out between proslavery
factions and abolitionists, sometimes resulting in blood-
shed and death. Abolitionist Senator Charles Sumner,
while seated at his desk in the U.S. Senate, was badly
beaten with a cane by Congressman Preston Brooks of
South Carolina. Brooks claimed that Sumner had
insulted slaveholders in a speech he had made about
"Bleeding Kansas," where slavery and abolition forces
were taking up arms over the issue.

New Orleans, although far removed from the
North, still felt the mounting tension. Many in the city
shared the sentiments expressed in 1822 by a group of
whites in Charleston, South Carolina: "The superior
condition of the free persons of color excites discontent
among our slaves, who continually have before their
eyes, persons of the same color, many of whom they
had known in slavery . . . freed from the control of
masters, working where they please, going whither they
please . . . [and, seeing them] the slave pants for
liberty."

As one of the major ports for slave ships, New
Orleans had much to be worried about. Since color was
the main feature distinguishing a slave, there was little
means of telling free blacks from slaves—or runaways.
Something had to be done, the white leaders felt,
and as a free black in New Orleans, Rillieux felt the
problem most keenly.

Increasingly Rillieux found his freedom curtailed.
He himself was a wealthy, influential man, yet, because

of his color, he was restricted from calling on or visiting his white peers unless he was invited to do so. The final blow came in 1854 when he was required by law to carry a pass in order to travel freely about the city. He decided to leave the United States forever.

On his return to France, Rillieux intended to continue in the sugar-refining trade, utilizing the invention that had earned him great wealth in America. But the refining of sugar wasn't a key industry in Europe as it had been in New Orleans and the Europeans were indifferent to Rillieux's invention. After several attempts at interesting them in his system, Rillieux gave up and devoted the next ten years of his life to deciphering Egyptian hieroglyphics. Eventually he was able to capture the attention of the Europeans and his process was adapted to the refining of the sugar beet which, like the sugar cane of the United States, was the main source of European sugar. Again production costs were dramatically reduced, production increased, and Rillieux added to his wealth.

France's gain was America's loss. Had Norbert Rillieux remained in the United States and been free to pursue his interests, there is no way to tell how many other labor-saving devices he might have invented that would have had as great an impact as his sugar-refining process. His interests were numerous and varied. Before he left for Paris, for example, Rillieux had submitted to the city authorities of New Orleans a complicated proposal for a sewerage system for the city, which was turned down. As it is, Rillieux's name is immortalized for his sugar-refining system, which is utilized around

A medal with the likeness of Norbert Rillieux, who left the United States for France in order to live in freedom and dignity. (Moorland-Spingarn Research Center, Howard University)

the world and has since been adapted to the refining of other products such as evaporated milk and cocoa.

While Norbert Rillieux was able to escape the mounting tensions between proslavery and antislavery factions in the United States, most blacks did not have his advantages, being tied to America either by poverty or the chains of slavery. With the firing on Fort Sumter in 1861, the Civil War began, however, and, with it, upheaval and turmoil swept across the nation, to last even after the war was ended in 1865. Inventive minds turned their attentions to ways to establish equality—or merely to stay alive amidst the conflict. Many blacks begged to join the forces fighting for freedom, but it was not until President Abraham Lincoln issued the Emancipation Proclamation in 1863 that the United States armed forces were permitted to accept blacks, slave and free, in their companies (before 1863, although there were black regiments in Louisiana, Missouri, and South Carolina, they had no official standing with the Union Army).

As the war progressed, the issues of freedom and equality led to a number of legal changes in the North. Illinois and California dropped their "Black Laws" denying equal rights, and Illinois repealed a law that punished blacks for merely entering the state. All over the North changes were occurring and, with the war's end, freedom was granted to those who had suffered the shackles of slavery. But freedom and the changing of laws did not necessarily mean equality in fact, and in the peace that followed the Civil War quiet battles were being fought to secure the benefits of freedom for which both black and white had fought: the right to vote; the right to an education; the right to own land, and more. One benefit to blacks that was quickly reinstated was the right to file and obtain patents on the products of their ingenuity. This would lead to a veritable flood of patent applications from black inventors throughout the United States in the latter half of the nineteenth century.

chapter
5

JAN MATZELIGER

AND

"THE REAL McCOY"

*B*y 1870 the constraints imposed before and
during the Civil War on the patenting of inventions by blacks had been lifted. Patent applications by blacks increased from a trickle to a stream to a
rushing flood over the latter half of the nineteenth
century. The biased views previously held against
blacks—that they were intellectually inferior, childlike
and so on—were slowly eroding. In 1894, Congressman
George H. Murray, a former slave and a champion of
black education, told his colleagues in the House of
Representatives:

> *We [blacks] have proven in almost every line*
> *that we are capable of doing what other people*
> *can do. We have proven that we can work as*

*much and as well as other people. We have proven
that we can learn as well as other people. . . .*

*I hold in my hand a statement prepared by
one of the assistants in the Patent Office, showing
the inventions that have been made by colored
men within the past few years. . . .*

*This statement shows that colored men have
taken out patents upon almost everything from
a cooking stove to a locomotive. Patents have been
granted to colored men for inventions and improvements in the workshop, on the farm, in the
factory, on the railroad, in the mine, in almost
every department of labor, and some of the most
important improvements that go to make up that
great motive power of modern industrial machinery, the steam engine, have been produced by
colored men. . . .*

After concluding his address, Congressman Murray
then read into *The Congressional Record* a list of ninety-
two patents received by black inventors; eight of those
patents were held by the Congressman himself.

Black inventors were making an impact upon
American society that could hardly be ignored, and
one such inventor, Jan Ernst Matzeliger (1852–1889),
created a device that was so complex and advanced it
could hardly be understood, let alone ignored. His
invention affected everyone in their daily comings and
goings, yet few knew his name nor how he had improved their lives.

In 1876 Jan Ernst Matzeliger arrived in Lynn,
Massachusetts, from his native Dutch Guiana. The son
of a Dutch father and Surinamese mother, Matzeliger

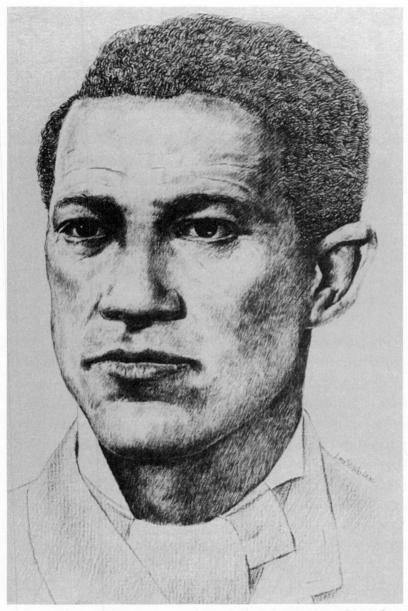

*J*an Ernst Matzeliger invented a shoe-lasting machine that
revolutionized the shoe industry, created thousands of jobs,
and cut shoe prices in half. (Moorland-Spingarn Research
Center, Howard University)

looked to the United States for opportunity and wealth. Although he spoke little English, he was interested in mechanical things and was able to obtain a job in a shoe factory. There he became aware of the problem involved in "lasting" shoes.

For years, various inventors had tackled the problem of shoe lasting: shaping the upper leather portion of a shoe over the last (the shoe form) and attaching this leather to the bottom of the shoe, the sole. Various inventors had contrived crude shoemaking machines but the final step in shoemaking, lasting, could not—it seemed—be done by machine; it had to be done by hand. Or so everyone thought.

Metzeliger secretly worked on the problem for ten years and, during that time, made a number of machines that he thought might last shoes, but each one ultimately failed. Finally, in 1882, he built a machine that did indeed last shoes, but then he ran into another, unexpected problem. When he applied for a patent and sent his diagrams to the United States Patent Office, his machine was too complex for the officials to understand. An official from the Patent Office had to be sent from Washington, D.C., to look at Matzeliger's original model, and on March 20, 1883, Jan E. Matzeliger was granted Patent number 274,207.

Almost at once, Matzeliger's machine revolutionized the shoemaking industry. His machine increased production tremendously while, at the same time, cutting production costs and, subsequently, the retail price of shoes.

While Matzeliger's name became famous in the

*M*atzeliger's shoe-lasting machine, for which he received a patent in 1883. (Moorland-Spingarn Research Center, Howard University)

shoemaking industry, his own life changed little. He had arrived in Massachusetts alone and friendless and, for much of his life, he remained lonely. Initially he applied for membership in several churches, but was denied because of his color. He finally joined a young adult group where he made some friends, but he never married, devoting the majority of his free time to developing his shoe-lasting machine. Nor did he get an opportunity to enjoy fully the fruits of his labors and self-denial. Six years after he patented his machine, in 1889, Jan Ernst Matzeliger died of tuberculosis.

One contemporary of Matzeliger's who did live to enjoy the fruits of his own inventiveness — and whose name was to become a household word — was Elijah McCoy. McCoy's name is still remembered today and has become synonymous with the ideas of perfection and quality. When we say that something is "the real McCoy," we are remembering Elijah McCoy whether we are aware of it or not.

Elijah McCoy (1843–1929) was born on May 2, 1843, in Colchester, Ontario, Canada, the son of two runaway slaves, fugitives who had escaped from Kentucky by way of the Underground Railroad. After the Civil War, Elijah and his parents returned to the United States, settling down near Ypsilanti, Michigan. There Elijah attended school and worked in a machine shop.

McCoy, even as a boy, was fascinated with machines and tools. He was fortunate to have been born into an era that suited him perfectly, a time when newer and better machines were being invented — the age of the machine. Following the footsteps of steam was that new

energy source, electricity, which opened up even more
opportunities for the inventive mind.

McCoy's interest only deepened with the emer-
gence of each new device. He decided to go to Edin-
burgh, Scotland, where the bias against his color was
not so evident, and serve an apprenticeship in mechanical engineering. After finishing his apprenticeship,
McCoy returned to the United States a mechanical
engineer, eager to put his skills to work. But companies
at that time were reluctant to hire a black man to fill
such a highly skilled position. Prejudice was strong and
the myth that blacks were intellectually inferior to
whites persisted. Companies felt that McCoy could not
possibly be as skilled as he claimed to be and, even if he
were, the white workers he might have to supervise
would never take orders from a black man. The only
job he was able to find was as a fireman on the Michigan Central Railroad.

The job of fireman was hardly one that required
the sophisticated skills McCoy had obtained. His duties
consisted of fueling the firebox of the engine to "keep
the steam up" and oiling the engine. The way train and
other types of engines were built meant that it was
necessary to stop the train periodically—or to shut
down whatever engine was being used—so the moving
parts could be lubricated. If the engines were not oiled,
the parts would wear out quickly or friction would
cause the parts to heat up, causing fires. Hand-lubricat-
ing engines was an inefficient but necessary procedure.

Many men or women, when faced with a repetitive,
essentially mindless task, might sink into an unthinking

lethargy, doing only that which is required of them and no more, but this was not true of Elijah McCoy. He did his job—oiling the engines—but that job led him to become interested in the problems of lubricating any kind of machinery that was in motion. For two years he worked on the problem on his own time in his own homemade machine shop. His initial idea was to manufacture the machines with canals cut into them with connecting devices between their various parts to distribute the oil throughout the machines while they were running. He wanted to make lubrication automatic.

Finally McCoy came up with what he called "the lubricating cup," or "drip cup." The lubricating cup was a small container filled with oil, with a stop cock to regulate the flow of oil into the parts of a moving machine. The lubricating or drip cup seemed an obvious invention, yet no one had thought of it before McCoy; it has since been described as the "key device in perfecting the overall lubrication system used in large industry today." With a drip cup installed, it was no longer necessary to shut down a machine in order to oil it, thus saving both time and money. McCoy received his patent for it on July 12, 1872.

The drip cup could be used on machinery of all types and it was quickly adopted by machine manufacturers everywhere. Of course, there were imitators, but their devices were not as effective or efficient as McCoy's. It soon became standard practice for an equipment buyer to inquire if the machine contained "the real McCoy." So commonly was this expression used that it soon spread outside the machine industry and came to have the general meaning of the "real thing," of perfection. Nowadays if someone states they want "the real McCoy," it is taken to mean that they want the genuine article, the best, not a shoddy imitation. In 1872, of course, Elijah McCoy could not foresee that his name would soon become associated with the idea of perfection. All he knew was that the thing worked and worked well on machinery of all types.

The lubrication of machinery fascinated McCoy and he continued to work in that area. In 1892 he invented and patented a number of devices for lubricating locomotive engines. These inventions were used in all western railroads and on steamers plying the Great Lakes. Eventually McCoy would invent a total of twenty-three lubricators for different kinds of equipment and, in 1920, he applied his system to air brakes on vehicles.

During his lifetime, Elijah McCoy was awarded over fifty-seven patents and became known as one of the most prolific black inventors of the nineteenth century. In addition to his patents on various kinds of lubricating systems, he also received patents for such "homey" objects as an ironing table (a forerunner of today's ironing board), a lawn sprinkler, a steam dome and a dope cup (a cup for administering medicine). He eventually founded the Elijah McCoy Manufacturing Company in Detroit, Michigan, to develop and sell his inventions.

Until his death in 1929, McCoy continued working and inventing, sometimes patenting two or three new

Elijah McCoy, for whom the term "the real McCoy" was coined. (Moorland-Spingarn Research Center, Howard University)

devices a year. Today, although many may not know who he was or what he did, his name remains to remind us of the idea of quality, and the steady, ceaseless roar of machinery is a paean to his inventiveness.

chapter
6

"ELECTRIFYING INVENTORS":
LEWIS LATIMER AND
GRANVILLE T. WOODS

*T*he second half of the nineteenth century witnessed an explosion of inventiveness, much of
which centered around the new power source—
electricity. Electricity was clean, efficient, and able to be
adapted to an infinite variety of uses. It was the "modern wonder" that was to change everyday life in hundreds of ways.

In the history of the development of electrical
devices, every schoolchild is taught the names of such
men as Thomas A. Edison and Alexander Graham
Bell, but these men were not the only ones contributing
to the growing industrialization and electrification of
America. Of equal importance were two black inventors
whose contributions rank beside those of Edison and

Bell: Lewis Latimer (1848–1928) and Granville T.
Woods (1856–1910).

"The greatest electrician in the world," "the greatest colored inventor in the history of the race, and
equal, if not superior, to any inventor in the country,"
said the *Catholic Tribune* in 1886. The praise and acco-
lades heaped upon Granville T. Woods, known as the
"Black Edison," were many and were justly deserved.
But they were also hard-earned.

Granville T. Woods was born in Columbus, Ohio,
on April 23, 1856. His formal early schooling ended at
the age of ten when he was forced by circumstances to
go to work, but he never stopped learning or applying
what he had learned to the world around him. After he
left school, Woods first worked in a machine shop. His
basic interest and knowledge of mechanics was increased by jobs on a Missouri railroad in 1872, and a
steel rolling mill in 1874. The practical knowledge he
gained in these jobs was impressive and it enabled him
to qualify to study mechanical engineering at an east-
ern college in 1876.

After his college training, Woods went to work as
an engineer on a British steamer, the *Ironsides,* in 1878,
and in 1880 drove a steam locomotive on the D & S
Railroad. Woods's background and education suited
him for more responsible jobs, but, because of his
color, he was refused promotion again and again. Not
only did he have to face a lack of advancement in his
job because of his color, but there was no means by
which he could ever achieve a position of influence

while working for others. Woods recognized the inevitable; he was never going to succeed if he was dependent upon the whims and biases of others. In 1884, therefore, he formed the Woods Railway Telegraph Company in Cincinnati, Ohio, and began his career as an inventor. In 1887, he patented his Synchronous Multiplex Railway Telegraph, a system designed to avert railroad accidents by keeping the trains in touch with each other by telegraph.

Granville T. Woods utilized his background and directed his talents toward inventions for the railroad and electrical industries and, over the next thirty years, secured more than fifty patents. An article that appeared in *Cosmopolitan Magazine* in 1895 mentions some of his achievements:

> *He is the inventor of a telephone which he sold to the Bell Telephone Company, and of a system of telegraphing from moving railway trains, which was successfully tried on the New Rochelle branch of the New Haven Railroad in 1885. Three years ago [in 1892], an electric railway system of his invention was operated at Coney Island [New York]. It had neither exposed wires, secondary batteries, nor a slotted way. The current was taken from iron blocks placed at intervals of twelve feet between the rails, in which, by an ingenious arrangement of magnets and switches, the current was turned on to the blocks only as they were successively covered by the cars.*
>
> *The most remarkable invention of Mr. Woods is for the regulation of electric motors. In almost all applications of electric power it is necessary at*

> *times to control the speed of the motors without*
> *changing the loads or disturbing the voltage at*
> *the source of supply. This has usually been done*
> *by introducing large dead resistances in series*
> *with the motors. These quickly become hot, and*
> *are extremely wasteful of electricity. Mr. Woods*
> *has, by his improvements, reduced the size of these*
> *resistances, so as to materially lessen the losses*
> *by them, and to remove other objectionable*
> *features. . . .*

In addition to those mentioned, Woods obtained patents on the automatic air brake in 1902, which he
subsequently sold to George Westinghouse. He also
patented a steam boiler furnace (1884), and an incuba-
tor (1900).

Woods's path was not an easy one, however. He was
forced to sue the Edison Company twice for patent
infringement. Each time he was able to prove success-
fully that he had earlier rights to inventions claimed by
Thomas Edison. After the second case, Edison offered
Woods a position with his company. Woods declined,
preferring to be his own boss.

Lewis Howard Latimer, on the other hand, did
choose to work for Thomas A. Edison and was one of
the Edison Pioneers, the early group of inventors who
worked for Edison. On Latimer's death in 1928, the
Pioneers issued this statement detailing his life:

> *Mr. Latimer was born at Chelsea, Massa-*
> *chusetts, September 4, 1848. . . . At the age of*
> *sixteen he enlisted in the Naval service of the*

*Federal Government, serving as a "landsman" on
the U.S.S. Massasoit from which he was honor-
ably discharged in 1865, when he returned to
Boston and secured employment as an office boy
in the office of Messrs. Crosby and Gould, patent
solicitors. In this office he became interested in
drafting and gradually perfected himself to such a
degree as to become their chief draftsman. . . . It
was Mr. Latimer who executed the drawings and
assisted in preparing the applications for the
telephone patents of Alexander Graham Bell. In
1880, he entered the employ of Hiram S. Maxim,
Electrician of the United States Electric Lighting
Co., then located at Bridgeport, Connecticut. It
was while in this employ that Mr. Latimer suc-
cessfully produced a method of making carbon
filaments for the Maxim electric incandescent
lamp, which he patented. His keen perception of
the possibilities of the electric light and kindred
industries resulted in his being the author of
several other inventions. . . . In 1884, he became
associated with the Engineering Department of
the Edison Electric Light company. . . .*

*He was of the colored race, the only one in
our organization, and was one of those to respond
to the initial call that led to the formation of the
Edison Pioneers, January 24, 1918. Broadmind-
edness, versatility in the accomplishment of
things intellectual and cultural, a linguist, a
devoted husband and father, all were characteris-
tic of him, and his genial presence will be missed
from our gatherings.*

Lewis Latimer, the son of a fugitive slave from
Virginia, was born on September 4, 1848. His child-

hood in Chelsea was hard; his father disappeared and
Latimer was forced to work to help support his family.
He sold copies of William Lloyd Garrison's *The Liberator*
on the streets, both earning money and supporting the
abolitionist cause. In his teenage years, Latimer and his
brother William were sent to a farm school. Born and
raised in the city, they despised the farm school, ran
away and, at the age of fifteen, Latimer enlisted in the
Union navy.

After the Civil War, Latimer began work at Crosby
and Gould. While working there, he made the acquaintance of Alexander Graham Bell, who was teaching
sign language to the deaf at a nearby school. Bell was
keenly interested in sign language as his wife was a
deaf-mute and he developed the telephone from his
work on a device to improve his wife's hearing. When
Bell needed assistance in preparing his patent applications, Latimer helped his friend, executing the drawings and helping to fill out the application forms.

Latimer's acquaintance with and employment by
Hiram S. Maxim led to his name becoming well-known
in the world of electrical invention. After Latimer
invented the first electric light with a carbon filament,
Maxim, along with a man named Charles Weston, set
up factories to manufacture Latimer's lamps. Latimer
even learned French so that the instructions for his
lamps would be clearly understood in the French-
speaking parts of Canada where many of his lamps
were sold. His life now included a great deal of travel as
he supervised the installation of his system of lighting
in New York, Philadelphia, Montreal, and London for

the Maxim-Weston Electric Company. Charles Weston, co-owner of the company and a good friend of Latimer's, would later establish the Westinghouse Company.

Latimer enjoyed his work with the company, but in 1883, when Thomas Edison asked Latimer to join his new company, he couldn't refuse. Initially Latimer was assigned to the engineering department; later he was transferred to the legal department. He worked on drafting plans for future patents and established himself as an expert legal witness in suits concerning patent abuse and infringement. It is even likely he was involved in preparing the suit between Granville T. Woods and the Edison Company. During this time, in 1890 Latimer also wrote the first textbook on electric lighting.

Latimer was not wholly absorbed in his work, however. In addition to his responsibilities with Edison, he took the time to help those less fortunate than himself, teaching mechanical drawing and English to recent immigrants to America. He was also an accomplished poet, musician, author, and artist. After his retirement, he published a volume of his poetry and devoted himself to the study of literature.

Both Granville T. Woods and Lewis H. Latimer were men of vision, men who could see the future inherent in electricity and who achieved recognition in that field. But many black inventors after the Civil War were denied recognition for their efforts. Too often they found that people wouldn't accept their inventions when it was learned that they were black. One

*L*ewis Howard Latimer invented the first electric light with *a carbon filament.* (Winifred L. Norman)

result of this bias was that many black inventors concealed their identities.

In 1900, Henry E. Baker, Assistant Examiner of the United States Patent Office, a black man himself, made an exhaustive study of the patent records to uncover black inventors and give them at least a small amount of recognition. He found between 800 and 1,200 patents that were assigned before the year 1913 to men he identified as colored.

Baker's list includes these inventions patented by Negroes before 1900: a jet-propulsion balloon; a railroad crossing switch; an electric lamp; a self-setting animal trap; a telephone system; combination seed planter and fertilizer distributor; letter box; window cleaner; gauge; guitar; printing press; lifesaving device for ships; folding chair; fountain pen; safety gate for bridges; a spring gun; a rapid-fire naval gun; bicycle; steam boiler.

The inventors of these devices, many forced to hide their true identities, still patented them, clinging to the same kind of hope and pride in their work of which Lewis Latimer wrote in one of his poems, *Hope:*

> *The two fortresses which are the*
> *last to yield in the human*
> *heart, are hope and pride.*

> *Hope springs eternal in the*
> *human breast, and is as*
> *necessary to life as the act of*
> *breathing.*

*For who would live if life held no
     allurements?*

*There must be vistas flying out
     beyond, that promise more
     than present conditions yield.*

chapter
7

LADIES
OF
INVENTION

*B*efore the Civil War, the place of the black
woman in America was at the bottom of the
social scale. In addition to working as field
hands or domestics within the master's house, black
female slaves were often purchased for breeding. The
Charleston, South Carolina, *City Gazette,* for example,
ran an advertisement placed by a man who was selling
a group of slaves that said: "They were purchased for
stock breeding Negroes, and to any planter who particularly wanted them for that purpose, they are a very
choice and desirable gang."

While the lot of the black woman was often of the
most debased sort, many had an admirable tenacity
and strength. Many, both secretly and openly, sup-

ported the abolitionist cause and, during the Civil War, worked in hospitals and camps to aid the Union.

For all black slaves, education was a commodity to be desired and passed on, for it could be a way to escape. Many black women ran secret schools. In Mississippi, for example, Milla Granson, a slave, conducted a midnight school for several years. She had been taught to read and write by the children of her former master in Kentucky, an indulgent man, and "in her little school hundreds of slaves benefited from her learning." For men and women, education was a secret freedom in the midst of slavery.

After the Civil War, black men and women continued to seek education. Education for black women was not a luxury, as it often was for white women. Rather, it was intended to train them for a profession, some sort of livelihood. More women in general, both black and white, were turning to business and industry for jobs rather than merely accepting the role of domestic servant. Often these new jobs were not challenging and were onerous in the extreme, but there was in them a sense of independence not found in a life of service. The machine age had created a slot for the working woman. It was felt that she was well-suited to factory work: She could tolerate, better than man, the monotonous, repetitive labor dictated by machines. However, the era of the late nineteenth and early twentieth centuries was a time in which such stereotypes were being challenged and, often, overturned.

One result of the increased number of women in

the workplace was a desire on their part to be on an equal footing with men. Not only were suffragette groups demanding the vote and growing more vocal every day, but women across the country began to enter the business world as employers rather than employees—and women were daring to enter the invention arena.

The number of recorded black women inventors is small and little is known about them. The inventions they created often revolved around or grew out of the necessities of their work or living arrangements. One of the first known black women inventors was Sarah Goode who in 1886 invented the folding cabinet bed. In 1892, Sarah Boone invented the ironing board, a device that is still in use today although Boone is not often remembered as its creator. Julia Hammond patented a device to hold yarn for knitting in 1896, and Archia Ross patented at least three inventions, including a rack to keep trousers from wrinkling in 1899. Claytonia Dorticus, who ran a photography studio in Newton, New Jersey, obtained a number of patents on inventions dealing with photography, among which were a machine for embossing photos (1895) and a photographic print wash (1875). In addition to her inventions dealing with photography, she also patented a device for applying coloring liquids to the sides of shoe soles or the heels (1895). However, perhaps the best remembered and most successful of the black women inventors was Sarah Breedlowe Walker (1867–1919) who is better known as Madam C. J. Walker.

Madam C. J. Walker was one of the first women in

America, black or white, to become a self-made millionaire. Sarah Breedlowe was born in Louisiana in 1867, the daughter of ex-slaves. She was orphaned at the age of six, married at the age of fourteen, and widowed at twenty when her husband was killed by a lynch mob. With her young daughter, Lelia, Sarah McWilliams moved to St. Louis where she earned a living by taking in laundry. Noticing that her hair was falling out, she experimented with all sorts of products, but none worked. Then, as she later told it, a black man came to her in a dream and gave her a secret formula for growing hair. She never revealed the formula, but it is said that the secret ingredient was sulfur.

In 1905, she moved to Denver and there met and married a man named C. J. Walker, who helped her to advertise and promote her product, which she called Madam C. J. Walker's Hair Grower. The marriage did not last, but Madam Walker's business did, and she developed more hair care products, including softeners and conditioners. Eventually, she created an entire Walker System of hair care.

While Madam Walker had little formal schooling, she had an innate talent for business and set up her manufacturing company efficiently and effectively. She organized her agents into clubs, trained operatives in her system, sold franchises, and provided the equipment needed to operate them. From her original hair-care system she expanded into an entire line of cosmetics for black women, a market almost ignored by white cosmetic manufacturers. Within a few years, the Madam C. J. Walker Manufacturing Company in Indi-

ana was a huge industry paying over $200,000 annually
to its personnel and including a school to train
salespeople.

From being a poor laundress, Madam Walker had
now progressed to the positions of president of a thriv-
ing company and a millionairess. Despite her success,
however, she was a pleasant, kindly person with an
interest in those less fortunate than herself. She supported many charitable causes and founded a girls'
academy in West Africa, providing it with a $100,000
grant.

The story of Madam Walker's success soon cap-
tured the interest of the newspapers and numerous
articles about her appeared, detailing both her business
and social life. Her success was well deserved and she
enjoyed it. She built herself a $250,000 mansion (an
enormous cost at that time), the Villa Lewaro, in Ir-
vington in upstate New York. She furnished it lavishly;
among her many showpieces were a gold-plated piano,
a $60,000 pipe organ, Hepplewhite furniture, Persian
rugs, and huge oil paintings. Villa Lewaro became one
of the showplaces of the "gilded age," and was visited
by some of the most prominent blacks of the time.

Although Madam C. J. Walker's life is a story of
overwhelming success, black women everywhere were
breaking out of the subservient positions in which they
had labored until long after the Civil War. Their efforts
were spurred not only by the desire to succeed, but
also by the fact that a majority were the sole supporters
of their families and often the heads of their house-
holds. Madam Walker not only provided a commodity

*M*adam *C. J. Walker became the first black woman millionaire as a result of her hair-care products.* (Moorland-Spingarn Research Center, Howard University)

that black women wanted, she provided an inspiration that black women needed.

Encouraged by stories such as Madam Walker's, in 1896 the National Association of Colored Women was founded in Washington, D.C.; in 1900 it became affiliated with the National Council of Women. It established educational, temperance, and service departments, and supported many causes and legislative efforts, such as the suffrage movement. By 1911, there were 45,000 black women affiliated with the National Council of Women. Although there was much to be done and "miles to go," black women, by 1900, were a force to be reckoned with in all fields of endeavor, including the field of invention.

chapter
8

*"THE WIZARD
OF TUSKEGEE":
GEORGE WASHINGTON
CARVER*

*I*f Madam C. J. Walker served as a role model for success among black women and girls in the early twentieth century, her contemporary, George Washington Carver (1864–1943) more than fulfilled that same function for black men and boys. Much has been written on the gentle, devout "Wizard of Tuskegee," and deservedly so. Because of his many achievements, Carver moved from humble beginnings to become one of the truly great men of his time.

George Washington Carver was born into slavery in Diamond Grove, Missouri. In 1864, although the end of the Civil War was nearing, slaves were still regarded as property, to be used as their masters wished. When Carver was only an infant, he and his mother were kidnapped from his owner's plantation by a band of

slave raiders. His mother was sold and shipped away,
but Carver's master ransomed him in exchange for a
horse.

When the Civil War ended, Carver was alone; he
had no idea where his mother was in the confusion that
followed the Emancipation Proclamation and the free-
ing of the slaves. However, although he was alone, he
was strong and determined. By working as a field hand,
he was able to get a high school education. He had a
thirst for knowledge and knew he would never be
content to work only as a field hand. Despite hardship
and deprivation, he set out to obtain that knowledge,
working his way through Simpson College, where he
was the first black student to be admitted, and where,
among other things, he studied art. He then went on to
attend Iowa Agricultural College (now Iowa State University) and received a degree in agriculture in 1894.
His efforts were rewarded in 1896 when he was hired
by Booker T. Washington to teach and conduct research at Tuskegee Institute in Alabama.

Tuskegee Normal Institute had been founded in
1881 as an agricultural and industrial school for black
students, one of a number of such institutions for black
students to spring up after the Civil War. As Samuel J.
Barrows wrote in his article, "What the Southern Negro
Is Doing for Himself," in 1891:

> *Another remarkable illustration [of the*
> *interest in education] is furnished by the Tuskegee*
> *Normal School. This institution was started in*
> *1881 by a Hampton graduate, Mr. Booker T.*

*Washington, on a state appropriation of $2,000.
It has grown from 30 pupils to 450, with 31
teachers. During the last year 200 applicants had
to be turned away for want of room. Fourteen
hundred acres of land and fourteen school build-
ings form a part of the equipment. . . . All the
teachers are colored. Of the fourteen school build-
ings, eight have been erected, in whole or in
part, by the students. . . .*

When George Washington Carver arrived at Tuskegee, it was a bustling, rapidly growing school filled with
students eager to educate themselves and better their
lives and the lives of their families. He set about teaching these students and also began, in his small laboratory at the Institute, research that was to occupy his
life.

Carver set out to achieve a number of things with
his research. First, and perhaps most importantly, he
wished to bring the findings of his laboratory to the
land. With knowledge and research, he felt, crops
could be grown more quickly, soil utilized more effectively—"schooling" was to be an integral part of the
farm of the future. The second goal he wished to
achieve was to develop a variety of crops to be grown in
the South; "King Cotton" had dominated southern
agriculture long enough; it was time to diversify.
Carver set about not only developing new strains of
various crop plants, but also finding uses for these
plants, creating a market for them. During his years of
research, Carver found more than three hundred and
fifty uses for peanuts, sweet potatoes, and pecans. From

peanuts alone, Carver developed such seemingly unrelated products as meal, instant and dry coffee, bleach, tan remover, wood filler, metal polish, paper, ink, shaving cream, rubbing oil, linoleum, synthetic rubber, and plastics. For the sweet potato, Carver devised more than one hundred uses, from postage stamp glue to sweet potato flour which became an important food product during World War I. His success could be measured in dollars: by 1938, peanuts alone had become a two-hundred-million-dollar industry in the South.

Carver was not able to patent the new strains of plants he developed; it wasn't until 1930 that the U.S. Patent Office permitted plants to be patented. Because of his desire to help others, Carver patented only three of his products developed from the plants he researched. In 1923 he received Patent No. 1,522,176 for a new cosmetic for women, the basic ingredients of which were mashed peanuts mixed with water, a preservative, and perfume to form a thick cream. He also received two patents for paints and varnishes derived from the same source.

As the years passed, Carver became a well-known figure in the region. With his "moveable school" he would drive out into the surrounding Alabama fields in a mule-drawn wagon and show both farmers and his students how to enrich their soil through crop rotation and improve their crop yields by planting soybeans, peanuts, and sweet potatoes. These crops replaced minerals lost from the soil in growing cotton. Farmers no longer had to be enslaved to "King Cotton," the

*G*eorge Washington Carver in his lab at Tuskegee Institute. *In spite of all his innovative work, he only received three patents.* (Moorland-Spingarn Research Center, Howard University)

fickleness of the cotton market, or the destructiveness of the boll weevil. Thanks to George Washington Carver, the peanut and the sweet potato have become important beyond measure to the economy of the South.

Carver's students knew him as a gentle man who "would never embarrass you or get angry in public," but his fame was spreading beyond the circle of his students. In 1935 he became a collaborator in the U.S. Department of Agriculture's Bureau of Plant Industry, for which he wrote many scientific bulletins on topics ranging from plant diseases to plant uses. At one time he was asked to testify before Congress about his work. He was given fifteen minutes in which to talk; none of the Congressmen thought a talk about sweet potatoes and peanuts would need to take any longer than that. His talk, however, so interested them that he was allowed nearly two more hours to complete it.

Carver's genius sparked the interest of others. The Crown Prince of Sweden spent three weeks with him watching how he made things grow and learning the uses of the various plants. Thomas A. Edison tried to hire Carver but was gently refused. Henry Ford, of automotive fame, set up a special laboratory for Carver and visited him there often. Carver was visited at Tuskegee by scientists and scholars from around the world. In 1916, he was named a Fellow of the Royal Society in London, and, in 1923, received the Spingarn Medal for his work.

One would think that a man as busy as George Washington Carver would have no time for other interests, but he also enjoyed painting. As a young student, he had studied art at Simpson College in Iowa and, later, he would often paint to relax. While he was still at college his paintings were deemed good enough to garner the notice of others and, in fact, some of them were displayed at the Columbian Exposition in Chicago in 1893. A number of his paintings are hung in the Carver Museum at Tuskegee Institute.

As Carver advanced into old age, he took steps to ensure that the work he had started for the benefit of all men would continue after his death. In 1938 he gave $30,000 to establish the George Washington Carver Foundation. Its purpose was to develop uses for agricultural wastes and, as Carver had done all his life, develop food and other products from plants. At his death, Carver willed his estate to the Foundation to guarantee its continuance.

When George Washington Carver died in 1943, at the age of seventy-eight, the entire nation mourned him, led by President Franklin D. Roosevelt. Most people knew him only for his work, but those who had studied with him and worked with him remembered him as a gentle, devout, amiable, yet humble man. But whether one knew him or not, his work had an effect on the lives of all Americans, and on the South in particular, that continues today.

When George Washington Carver arrived at Tuskegee Institute in 1896, the economy of the South was depressed; the region was still struggling to recover from the ravages of the Civil War. With the slave trade gone, cotton was the main moneymaker for the South,

Carver was a source of inspiration for many scientists and inventors who came after him. (Moorland-Spingarn Research Center, Howard University)

but it was subject to the whimsy of the weather, insects, and the market. In addition, cotton plants leeched vital minerals from the soil, often leaving the soil too depleted to support further growing. George Washington Carver took what was at hand and set out to solve these problems. By the time of his death, the economy of the South had been turned around. Through his work with pecans, soybeans, sweet potatoes, and, of course, the peanut, Carver showed farmers how to restore their soil and diversify their crops. He had created a market for those crops by discovering new uses for them. He was, in essence, the saviour of the economy of the South and of southern agriculture.

George Washington Carver also unknowingly contributed another thing of great value to America. Through the examples of his life and his work he has served to stimulate young people to follow in his footsteps. His devotion to his work, and his success show what one can achieve. Many scientists and inventors who have come after Carver have looked back on his life as a source of inspiration for their own work.

Likewise, his life was a life of caring. Many years before Martin Luther King, Jr., asked his followers to meet hatred with love, Dr. Carver said, "No man can drag me down so low as to make me hate him." Carver was buried next to Booker T. Washington at Tuskegee. The inscription on his grave sums up his life fully: "He could have added fortune to fame, but caring for neither, he found happiness and honor in being helpful to the world."

chapter
9

*T*he year 1900 seemed to herald a new prosperity, a new life to many Americans. There had been no major upheaval since the Civil War and, to a majority of people, the phrase, "God's in his heaven and all is right with the world," did, indeed, seem true. "Laws are becoming more just, rulers humane," wrote one minister at the time. "Music is becoming sweeter and books wiser; homes are happier, and the individual heart becoming at once more just and more gentle." But beneath these middle-class self-congratulations lay many problems.

Blacks were still struggling against racial prejudice, inequality, and repressive local laws. As one black Congressman, George H. White, noted in his farewell speech to Congress in 1901, after enumerating the success and achievements of southern blacks:

> We have done it in the face of lynching, burning at the stake, with the humiliation of "Jim Crow" cars, the disfranchisement of our male citizens, slander and degradation of our women, with factories closed against us, no Negro permitted to be conductor on the railway cars, whether run through the streets of our cities or across the prairies of our great country, no Negro permitted to run as engineer on a locomotive, most of the mines closed against us.

When President Theodore Roosevelt entered the White House, he invited Booker T. Washington to dinner. Southern newspapers reacted with anger. "When Mr. Roosevelt sits down to dinner with a Negro," wrote the *New Orleans Times Democrat*, "he declares that the Negro is the social equal of the white man." And another newspaper ended its tirade against the event with, "White men of the South, how do you like it? . . . White women of the South, how do YOU like it?"

No, all was not "right with the world," yet the continuing prejudice did not keep black genuis from expressing itself. While George Washington Carver was quietly creating his agricultural miracles at Tuskegee, other black inventors were making their marks in a variety of arenas.

"Explosion!"
The men scrambled to escape from Tunnel Num-

ber Five, which lay five miles out and 282 feet under the chilling waters of Lake Erie and the Cleveland Waterworks. As men staggered out through the smoke and debris, the news spread: more than two dozen men were still trapped in the tunnel. It was July 25, 1916.

Rescue operations started immediately, but the men found that the tunnel was filled not only with smoke and dust, but also with pockets of natural gas. There was no way an unprotected man could venture into the tunnel without asphyxiating. It seemed to all that the situation was hopeless. Then someone remembered Garrett Morgan (1875–1963) who had recently been demonstrating his "gas inhalator" in Cleveland in an attempt to interest local manufacturers.

At two in the morning, Morgan and his brother, Frank, descended into Tunnel Number Five wearing Morgan's inhalators. Assisted by volunteers, Garrett and Frank Morgan labored as the sun rose, dragging unconscious men to the tunnel's elevator where they could be lifted to safety.

No inventor could have wished for better publicity for his invention. Nearly overnight orders from fire companies around the nation began to pour into Morgan's offices in Cleveland. He was asked to demonstrate his inhalator in many towns and cities. But then he encountered a problem.

When it was found that Garrett Morgan was black, orders for his inhalator dropped off or were cancelled. In the South, he was forced to employ white men to demonstrate his device. The foolishness of racial bias was well on the way to depriving the nation of one of the best safety devices then available. The advent of World War I, however, changed things a bit.

World War I was the first war in which poisonous gas was used as a weapon. The government looked at Morgan's inhalator and decided that, whatever the inventor's race, here was a device the soldiers on the battlefields of Europe desperately needed. The Morgan inhalator was transformed into the gas mask, saving the lives of thousands in combat.

The inhalator was not the only device Morgan invented. His first invention had been an improvement on the sewing machine that he had sold for $150. In 1923, Morgan came up with an invention that, although we are often unaware of it, affects our lives and safety every day: the automatic traffic signal. The stoplight hanging at the corner is there thanks to Garrett Morgan. Having established his reputation with his inhalator, Morgan was able to sell his traffic signal, not for the mere $150 he had received for his first invention, but for $40,000 to the General Electric Company.

Garrett Morgan had been born a poor boy in Paris, Kentucky, and had moved to Cleveland with his family when he was very young. When Morgan died in 1963, he was a successful businessman and inventor who had been awarded a gold medal by his adopted hometown, Cleveland, for his devotion to public safety.

While Morgan was striving to make life safer, another man was working to make our lives healthier. Percy Julian (1898–1975) was born in Montgomery, Alabama, the son of a railway clerk. Throughout his childhood, Julian's mother stressed to both him and his

*G*arrett Morgan invented two life-saving devices—a breathing mask, and the traffic light. (Moorland-Spingarn Research Center, Howard University)

brothers the value of a good education. After graduating from high school, he attended DePauw University in Greencastle, Indiana, where he worked his way through school, living in the attic of the fraternity house where he held the job of waiter. His hard work and sacrifices paid off, and in 1920 he graduated Phi Beta Kappa and was the valedictorian of his class. His mother was so impressed by how well he had done that she moved the rest of the family to Greencastle so that they too could attend DePauw.

After graduation, Julian spent several years teaching at Fisk and Howard Universities and West Virginia State College before attending Harvard and the University of Vienna where he received his doctorate. Julian then began teaching at DePauw and started the research that was to fill his life and make him the most famous black scientist of his time and the holder of eighty-six patents, some as sole inventor, some shared with his colleagues.

Julian's first discovery came in 1935 when he synthesized the drug physostigmine which is used in the treatment of glaucoma, a disease of the eye. His discoveries came to the notice of the Glidden Company where he eventually became the director of research and manager of fine chemicals. While at Glidden, Julian began researching the soybean. "Until the late thirties, Europe had a monopoly on the production of sterols. These sterols were extracted from the bile of animals at a cost of several hundred dollars a gram." Julian hoped to provide, from soybean oil, a substitute for the expensive sterols, and he was successful. "The

*D*r. *Percy Julian created drugs to treat glaucoma and arthritis, and secured a total of 86 patents.* (Moorland-Spingarn Research Center, Howard University)

method perfected by Dr. Julian in 1950 eventually lowered the cost of sterols to less than twenty cents a gram, and ultimately enabled millions of people suffering from arthritis to obtain relief through the use of cortisone, a sterol derivative."

In 1953, Julian founded his own company, the Julian Institute in Franklin Park, Illinois, and later, another in Mexico, devoted primarily to the production of sterols. His companies were successful almost immediately; in its second year of existence, Julian Institute showed a profit of $97,000. In 1961, the Institute was sold to Smith, Klein and French for several million dollars.

Percy Julian's life work helped to create the derivative drugs available to us today that ease suffering at a reasonable cost. He is not only remembered by other chemists in his field, but by his own university. The chemistry and mathematics building at DePauw University, where he had labored to get an education, is named for him.

chapter 10

MODERN

WIZARDS

*T*he twentieth century has witnessed a technological revolution seen in no other century. The very
way everyday life is conducted has been altered
dramatically since 1900. Radio, television, computers,
and even the exploration of space have become commonplace to us. Two World Wars, the Korean conflict,
and the war in Vietnam have changed the role of the
United States as a world power, and the weapons developed during these wars have changed the nature of war
itself. Even in the area of Civil Rights, change has been
dramatic, though hard-won. Whereas in 1900, when
Teddy Roosevelt invited Booker T. Washington to
dinner, he was derided and criticized, in 1965, another
president, Lyndon B. Johnson, was able to say to Congress, regarding inequality:

*The real hero of this struggle is the Ameri-
can Negro. His actions and protests, his courage
to risk safety and even to risk his life, have awak-
ened the conscience of this nation. His demonstra-
tions have been designed to call attention to
injustice, designed to stir reform. He has called
upon us to make good the promise of America.
And who among us can say that we would have
made the same progress were it not for his persist-
ent bravery, and his faith in American democ-
racy. . . .*

"The times they are a-changing," as the song of that
period said.

But for many people, the changes that have oc-
curred were and are unsettling because of their rapid-
ity. Many find it difficult to keep up with all the change
that has taken place in the twentieth century. One day,
a letter is sent through the U.S. Postal Service; the very
next day, it seems, in the interests of speed, that letter
is faxed. One instant, people are marveling over flying
across the country; the next, flying into space. While all
this change may seem unsettling, the majority feel that
it is exciting and, for the most part, beneficial.

The field of invention has flourished during the
twentieth century, although, with the growth of large
corporations, often the individual inventor or
researcher is overlooked. Under the terms of a majority
of corporation contracts, any new device or discovery
made by someone who is employed by a particular
company belongs to that corporation—and is often
patented by that corporation. But some individuals do

stand out, whether their discoveries were patented by themselves or by the companies for which they work.

Television, radio, and computers are commonplace objects in the world today. This is due, in part at least, to the work of Otis Boykin (born 1920). Boykin's first job was as a laboratory assistant testing automatic controls for airplanes. This led Boykin to a general interest in electronic control systems, and he soon developed an entire range of electrical devices, one a type of resistor that is now used commonly in radios, television, and computers. "He also developed a control unit for artificial heart stimulators [pacemakers], a variable resistor used in guided missiles, small components such as thick-film resistors for computers, a burglar-proof cash register, and a chemical air filter." Boykin's control systems have made available to us many of the modern innovations we take for granted today in our homes and in military use.

Another black inventor whose work has been utilized both commercially and militarily is George E. Alcorn (born 1942). An excellent student and athlete, Alcorn majored in physics at Occidental College in Los Angeles and, in 1963, received a master's degree in nuclear physics from Howard University. In summer jobs at North American Rockwell, he worked on the computer analysis of trajectories and orbital mechanics for various missile systems. He received his Ph.D. in atomic and molecular physics from Howard University in 1965.

After graduation, Alcorn began research into

semiconductors. Semiconductors are a class of solids, such as germanium or silicon, with low electrical conductivity. Alcorn's research led to a number of innovations dealing with semiconductors and eventually resulted in eight patents. Among his accomplishments are "work on secret projects concerning missile reentry and missile defense; the design and building of space instrumentation, atmospheric contaminant sensors, magnetic mass spectrometers, chemical ionization mass spectrometers for experiments in planetary life detection, development of new concepts in magnet design, and the invention of a new type of high x-ray spectrometer." Someday, if life *is* discovered on another planet, that discovery may be due to Alcorn's developments with spectrometers.

George E. Carruthers (born 1940) is also working to unveil the secrets of outer space. Carruthers was born and raised on Chicago's south side. At an early age, he developed a keen interest in astronomy and space. At the age of ten Carruthers built himself a telescope; this interest was to continue through high school and college. In 1964 he received his Ph.D. in physics from the University of Illinois and began working with the Navy as a researcher.

Carruthers' position with the Navy and his interest in space led naturally to working with the National Aeronautics and Space Administration (NASA) and with William Conway. With Conway, Carruthers developed the Apollo 16 lunar surface ultraviolet camera/spectrograph. Carruthers designed it and Conway adapted it for use on the lunar mission. As a result of his work, Carruthers received the NASA Exceptional Scientific Achievement medal.

Yet another black scientist who is aiming for the stars is Harrison Allen, Jr., who is a chemical engineer with NASA. Allen graduated from Cleveland State University and did graduate work at Case Western Reserve University. In his work for NASA, Allen has specialized in the development of high energy fuels for rockets, supersonic combustion, and solid rocket ignition. He holds a patent on the ignition of solid propellant rocket motors.

Boykin, Alcorn, Carruthers, and Allen are but four of the black men and women who are expanding our knowledge and improving our daily lives and who have helped open the world and space to mankind. They have been preceded in their inventiveness by a long and illustrious list of innovators who have tried to change the world for the better, each in different ways. Yet, although the means may have been different, all these men and women, and all inventors, share some things in common.

The art of invention is, basically, the art of problem-solving. The inventors described here, and all inventors, have the ability to *recognize* a problem when it presents itself, and the ability to seek a solution to that problem. Similarly, the inventions they devised filled needs that already existed or ended situations that frustrated people, or both. Lewis Temple, in the 1800's, saw the frustration the whalers felt on losing their catch. The whalers needed a better harpoon

which would end their frustration at losing whales.
Percy Julian saw the need for an arthritis medicine to
ease the suffering of thousands; as a medical researcher, he was all too familiar with the frustration felt
by physicians at not being able to treat people effectively. So he set about developing a sterol that was
inexpensive and effective.

These men and women have, through their crea-
tivity, ingenuity, and knowledge, brought about
changes that have been of enormous benefit to all
mankind. And because of their persistence in the face
of prejudice and inequality, black inventors today are
given the recognition and rewards their ingenuity justly
deserves and have paved the way for the inventor of
tomorrow.

appendix

INVENTIONS BY BLACKS 1834–1900

INVENTOR	INVENTION	DATE	PATENT
Abrams, W. B.	Hame attachment	Apr. 14, 1891	450,550
Allen, C. W.	Self-leveling table	Nov. 1, 1898	613,436
Allen, J. B.	Clothes line support	Dec. 10, 1895	551,105
Ancker Johnson, Betsy	Signal Generator	Nov. 22, 1966	3,287,659
Ashbourne, A. P.	Process for preparing coconut for domestic use	June 1, 1875	163,962
Ashbourne, A. P.	Biscuit cutter	Nov. 30, 1875	170,460
Ashbourne, A. P.	Refining coconut oil	July 27, 1880	230,518
Ashbourne, A. P.	Process of treating coconut	Aug. 21, 1877	194,287
Bailes, William	Ladder scaffold-support	Aug. 5, 1879	218,154
Bailey, L. C.	Combined truss and bandage	Sept. 25, 1883	285,545
Bailey, L. C.	Folding bed	July 18, 1899	629,286
Bailiff, C. O.	Shampoo headrest	Oct. 11, 1898	612,008
Ballow, W. J.	Combined hatrack and table	Mar. 29, 1898	601,422
Bayliss, R. G. & D. D. Emrick	Encapsulation process & its product	Feb. 2, 1971	3,565,818
Barnes, G. A. E.	Design for sign	Aug. 19, 1889	29,193
Beard, A. J.	Rotary engine	July 5, 1892	478,271
Beard, A. J.	Car-coupler	Nov. 23, 1897	594,059
Becket, G. E.	Letter box	Oct. 4, 1892	483,525
Bell, L.	Locomotive smoke stack	May 23, 1871	115,153
Bell, L.	Dough kneader	Dec. 10, 1872	133,823
Benjamin, L. W.	Broom moisteners and bridles	May 16, 1893	497,747
Benjamin, M. E.	Gong and signal chairs for hotels	July 17, 1888	386,286
Binga, M. W.	Street sprinkling apparatus	July 22, 1879	217,843
Blackburn, A. B.	Railway signal	Jan. 10, 1888	376,362
Blackburn, A. B.	Spring seat for chairs	Apr. 3, 1888	380,420
Blackburn, A. B.	Cash carrier	Oct. 23, 1888	391,577
Blair, Henry	Corn planter	Oct. 14, 1834	NA
Blair, Henry	Cotton planter	Aug. 31, 1836	NA
Blue, L.	Hand corn shelling device	May 20, 1884	298,937
Bluford, Sr. G. S.	Artillery Ammunition Training Round	Feb. 13, 1951	2,541,025
Booker, L. F.	Design rubber scraping knife	Mar. 28, 1899	30,404

INVENTOR	INVENTION	DATE	PATENT
Boone, Sarah	*Ironing board*	*Apr. 26, 1892*	*473,653*
Bowman, H. A.	*Making flags*	*Feb. 23, 1892*	*469,395*
Brooks, C. B.	*Punch*	*Oct. 31, 1893*	*507,672*
Brooks, C. B.	*Street-sweepers*	*Mar. 17, 1896*	*556,711*
Brooks, C. B.	*Street-sweepers*	*May 12, 1896*	*560,154*
Brooks, Hallstead and Page	*Street-sweepers*	*Apr. 21, 1896*	*558,719*
Brown, Henry	*Receptacle for storing and preserving papers*	*Nov. 2, 1886*	*352,036*
Brown, L. F.	*Bridle bit*	*Oct. 25, 1892*	*484,994*
Brown, O. E.	*Horseshoe*	*Aug. 23, 1892*	*481,271*
Brown & Latimer	*Water closets for railway cars*	*Feb. 10, 1874*	*147,363*
Bluford, Sr. G. S.	*Artillery Ammunition Training Round*	*Feb. 13, 1951*	*2,541,025*
Bundy, R.	*Signal generator*	*Jan. 26, 1960*	*2,922,924*
Burr, J. A.	*Lawn mower*	*May 9, 1899*	*624,749*
Burr, W. F.	*Switching device for railways*	*Oct. 31, 1899*	*636,197*
Burwell, W.	*Boot or shoe*	*Nov. 28, 1899*	*638,143*
Butler, R. A.	*Train alarm*	*June 15, 1897*	*584,540*
Butts, J. W.	*Luggage carrier*	*Oct. 10, 1899*	*634,611*
Byrd, T. J.	*Improvement in holders for reins for horses*	*Feb. 6, 1872*	*123,328*
Byrd, T. J.	*Apparatus for detaching horses from carriages*	*Mar. 19, 1872*	*124,791*
Byrd, T. J.	*Improvement in neck yokes for wagons*	*Mar. 19, 1872*	*124,790*
Byrd, T. J.	*Improvement in car couplings*	*Dec. 1, 1874*	*157,370*
Campbell, W. S.	*Self-setting animal trap*	*Aug. 30, 1881*	*246,369*
Cargill, B. F.	*Invalid cot*	*July 25, 1899*	*629,658*
Carrington, T. A.	*Range*	*July 25, 1876*	*180,323*
Carter, W. C.	*Umbrella stand*	*Aug. 4, 1885*	*323,397*
Carruthers, Geo. R.	*Image converter for Dect. Electromagnetic etc.*	*Nov. 11, 1969*	*3,478,216*
Carter, J. L. & M. Weiner & R. J. Youmans	*Distributed pulse forming network for magnetic modulator*	*Sept. 16, 1986*	*4,612,455*
Certain, J. M.	*Parcel carrier for bicycles*	*Dec. 26, 1899*	*639,708*
Cherry, M. A.	*Velocipede*	*May 8, 1888*	*382,351*
Cherry, M. A.	*Street car fender*	*Jan. 1, 1895*	*531,908*
Church, T. S.	*Carpet beating machine*	*July 29, 1884*	*302,237*
Clare, O. B.	*Trestle*	*Oct. 9, 1888*	*390,752*
Coates, R.	*Overboot for horses*	*Apr. 19, 1892*	*473,295*
Cook, G.	*Automatic fishing device*	*May 30, 1899*	*625,829*
Coolidge, J. S.	*Harness attachment*	*Nov. 13, 1888*	*392,908*
Cooper, A. R.	*Shoemaker's jack*	*Aug. 22, 1899*	*631,519*
Cooper, J.	*Shutter and fastening*	*May 1, 1883*	*276,563*
Cooper, J.	*Elevator device*	*Apr. 2, 1895*	*536,605*
Cooper, J.	*Elevator device*	*Sept. 21, 1897*	*590,257*

APPENDIX

INVENTOR	INVENTION	DATE	PATENT
Cornwell, P. W.	Draft regulator	Oct. 2, 1888	390,284
Cornwell, P. W.	Draft regulator	Feb. 7, 1893	491,082
Cralle, A. L.	Ice-cream mold	Feb. 2, 1897	576,395
Creamer, H.	Steam feed water trap	Mar. 17, 1895	313,854
Creamer, H.	Steam trap feeder	Dec. 11, 1888	394,463
Cosgrove, W. F.	Automatic stop plug for gas oil pipes	Mar. 17, 1885	313,993
Darkins, J. T.	Ventilation aid (variation)	Feb. 19, 1895	534,322
Davis, I. D.	Tonic	Nov. 2, 1886	351,829
Davis, W. D.	Riding saddles	Oct. 6, 1896	568,939
Davis, W. R., Jr.	Library table	Sept. 24, 1878	208,378
Deitz, W. A.	Shoe	Apr. 30, 1867	64,205
Dickinson, J. H.	Pianola	1899	NA
Dixon Jr. S. & T. R. AuCoin & R. J. Malik	Monolithic planar doped barrier limiter	Mar. 31, 1987	4,654,609
Dixon Jr. S. & R. J. Malik	Monolithic planar doped barrier subharmonic mixer	Jan. 7, 1986	4,563,773
Dorsey, O.	Door-holding device	Dec. 10, 1878	210,764
Dorticus, C. J.	Device for applying coloring liquids to sides of soles or heels of shoes	Mar. 19, 1895	535,820
Dorticus, C. J.	Machine for embossing photo	Apr. 16, 1895	537,442
Dorticus, C. J.	Photographic print wash	Apr. 23, 1875	537,968
Dorticus, C. J.	Hose leak stop	July 18, 1899	629,315
Downing, P. B.	Electric switch for railroad	June 17, 1890	430,118
Downing, P. B.	Letter box	Oct. 27, 1891	462,093
Downing, P. B.	Street letter box	Oct. 27, 1891	462,096
Dunnington, J. H.	Horse detachers	Mar. 16, 1897	578,979
Edmonds, T. H.	Separating screens	July 20, 1897	586,724
Elkins, T.	Dining, ironing table, and quilting frame combined	Feb. 22, 1870	100,020
Elkins, T.	Chamber commode	Jan. 9, 1872	122,518
Elkins, T.	Refrigerating apparatus	Nov. 4, 1879	221,222
Evans, J. H.	Convertible settees	Oct. 5, 1897	591,095
Faulkner, H.	Ventilated shoe	Apr. 29, 1890	426,495
Ferrell, F. J.	Steam trap	Feb. 11, 1890	420,993
Ferrell, F. J.	Apparatus for melting snow	May 27, 1890	428,670
Fisher, D.	Joiners' clamp	Apr. 20, 1875	162,281
Fisher, D. C.	Furniture castor	Mar. 14, 1876	174,794
Flemming, F., Jr.	Guitar (variation)	Mar. 3, 1886	338,727
Forten, J.	Sail control (described in Mass. newspaper)	1850	NA
Goode, Sarah E.	Folding cabinet bed	July 14, 1885	322,177
Gourdine, M. C.	Electrogas dynamic mtd. & apparatus	June 10, 1969	3,449,667

INVENTOR	INVENTION	DATE	PATENT
Grant, G. F.	*Golf tee*	*Dec. 12, 1899*	*638,920*
Grant, W.	*Curtain rod support*	*Aug. 4, 1896*	*565,075*
Gray, R. H.	*Bailing press*	*Aug. 28, 1894*	*525,203*
Gray, R. H.	*Cistern cleaners*	*Apr. 9, 1895*	*537,151*
Gregory, J.	*Motor*	*Apr. 26, 1887*	*361,937*
Grenon, H.	*Razor stropping device*	*Feb. 18, 1896*	*554,867*
Griffin, F. W.	*Pool table attachment*	*June 13, 1899*	*626,902*
Gunn, S. W.	*Boot or shoe (variation)*	*Jan. 16, 1900*	*641,642*
Haines, J. H.	*Portable basin*	*Sept. 28, 1897*	*590,833*
Hale, Wm.	*An improvement in airplanes*	*Apr. 7, 1925*	*1,563,278*
Hall, Lloyd A.	*Manuf. stable dry papain composition*	*March 15, 1949*	*2,464,200*
Hall, Lloyd A.	*Asphalt emulsion & manuf. thereof*	*Oct. 18, 1932*	*1,882,834*
Hall, Lloyd A.	*Sterilizing foodstuff*	*Feb. 8, 1938*	*2,107,697*
Hall, Lloyd A.	*Puncture sealing composition & manuf. thereof*	*Sept. 5, 1944*	*2,357,650*
Hammonds, J. F.	*Apparatus for holding yarn skeins*	*Dec. 15, 1896*	*572,985*
Harding, F. H.	*Extension banquet table*	*Nov. 22, 1898*	*614,468*
Harper, Solomon	*Electric Hair Treatment*	*Aug. 5, 1930*	*1,772,002*
Harper, Solomon	*Thermostatic Control Hair Curlers*	*Aug. 8, 1953*	*2,648,757*
Harper, S.	*Thermostatic Controlled Fur etc*	*Aug. 11, 1953*	*2,711,095*
Hawkins, J.	*Gridiron*	*Mar. 26, 1845*	*3,973*
Hawkins, R.	*Harness attachment*	*Oct. 4, 1887*	*370,943*
Headen, M.	*Foot power hammer*	*Oct. 5, 1886*	*350,363*
Hearness, R.	*Detachable car fender*	*July 4, 1899*	*628,003*
Hilyer, A. F.	*Water evaporator attachment for hot air registers*	*Aug. 26, 1890*	*435,095*
Hilyer, A. F.	*Registers*	*Oct. 14, 1890*	*438,159*
Holmes, E. H.	*Gage*	*Nov. 12, 1895*	*549,513*
Hunter, J. H.	*Portable weighing scales*	*Nov. 3, 1896*	*570,553*
Hyde, R. N.	*Composition for cleaning and preserving carpets*	*Nov. 6, 1888*	*392,205*
Jackson, B. F.	*Heating apparatus*	*Mar. 1, 1898*	*599,985*
Jackson, B. F.	*Matnx drying apparatus*	*May 10, 1898*	*603,879*
Jackson, B. F.	*Gas burner*	*Apr. 4, 1899*	*622,482*
Jackson, H. A.	*Kitchen table (variation)*	*Oct. 6, 1896*	*569,135*
Jackson, W. H.	*Railway switch*	*Mar. 9, 1897*	*578,641*
Jackson, W. H.	*Railway switch*	*Mar. 16, 1897*	*593,665*
Jackson, W. H.	*Automatic locking switch*	*Aug. 23, 1898*	*609,436*
Johnson, D.	*Rotary dining table*	*Jan. 15, 1888*	*396,089*
Johnson, D.	*Lawn mower attachment*	*Sept. 10, 1889*	*410,836*
Johnson, D.	*Grass receivers for lawn mowers*	*June 10, 1890*	*429,629*

INVENTOR	INVENTION	DATE	PATENT
Johnson, I. R.	*Bicycle frame*	*Oct. 10, 1899*	*634,823*
Johnson, P.	*Swinging chairs*	*Nov. 15, 1881*	*249,530*
Johnson, P.	*Eye protector*	*Nov. 2, 1880*	*234,039*
Johnson, W.	*Egg beater*	*Feb. 5, 1884*	*292,821*
Johnson, W.	*Velocipede*	*June 20, 1899*	*627,335*
Johnson, W. A.	*Paint vehicle*	*Dec. 4, 1888*	*393,763*
Johnson, W. H.	*Overcoming dead centers*	*Feb. 4, 1896*	*554,223*
Johnson, W. H.	*Overcoming dead centers*	*Oct. 11, 1898*	*612,345*
Jones, F. M.	*Ticket dispensing machine*	*June 27, 1939*	*2,163,754*
Jones, F. M.	*Air conditioning unit*	*July 12, 1949*	*2,475,841*
Jones, F. M.	*Two-cycle gasoline engine*	*Nov. 28, 1950*	*2,523,273*
Jones, F. M.	*Starter generator*	*July 12, 1949*	*2,475,842*
Jones, F. M.	*Thermostat and temperature control system*	*Feb. 23, 1960*	*2,926,005*
Jones & Long	*Caps for bottles*	*Sept. 13, 1898*	*610,715*
Joyce, J. A.	*Ore bucket*	*Apr. 26, 1898*	*603,143*
Julian, Hubert	*Airplane safety device*	*May 24, 1921*	*1,379,264*
Julian, Percy L.	*Preparation of cortisone*	*Aug. 10, 1954*	*2,752,339*
Julian, P. C. et al.	*Recovery of sterols*	*Oct. 22, 1940*	*2,718,971*
Latimer, L. H.	*Lamp fixture*	*Aug. 10, 1910*	*968,787*
Latimer, L. H.	*Manufacturing carbons*	*June 17, 1882*	*252,386*
Latimer, L. H.	*Apparatus for cooling and disinfecting*	*Jan. 12, 1886*	*334,078*
Latimer, L. H.	*Locking racks for hats, coats, and umbrellas*	*Mar. 24, 1896*	*557,076*
Latimer & Nichols	*Electric lamp*	*Sept. 13, 1881*	*247,097*
Latimer & Tregoning	*Globe support for electric lamps*	*Mar. 21, 1882*	*255,212*
Lavalette, W.	*Printing press (variation)*	*Sept. 17, 1878*	*208,208*
Lee, H.	*Animal trap*	*Feb. 12, 1867*	*61,941*
Lee, J.	*Kneading machine*	*Aug. 7, 1894*	*524,042*
Lee, J.	*Bread crumbing machine*	*June 4, 1895*	*540,553*
Leslie, F. W.	*Envelope seal*	*Sept. 21, 1897*	*590,325*
Lewis, A. L.	*Window cleaner*	*Sept. 27, 1892*	*483,359*
Lewis, E. R.	*Spring gun*	*May 3, 1887*	*362,096*
Linden, H.	*Piano truck*	*Sept. 8, 1891*	*459,365*
Little, E.	*Bridle-bit*	*Mar. 7, 1882*	*254,666*
Loudin, F. J.	*Sash fastener*	*Dec. 12, 1892*	*510,432*
Loudin, F. J.	*Key fastener*	*Jan. 9, 1894*	*512,308*
Love, J. L.	*Plasterers' hawk*	*July 9, 1895*	*542,419*
Love, J. L.	*Pencil sharpener*	*Nov. 23, 1897*	*594,114*
Marshall, T. J.	*Fire extinguisher (variation)*	*May 26, 1872*	*125,063*
Marshall, W.	*Grain binder*	*May 11, 1886*	*341,599*
Martin, W. A.	*Lock*	*July 23, 1889*	*407,738*
Martin, W. A.	*Lock*	*Dec. 30, 1890*	*443,945*
Matzeliger, J. E.	*Mechanism for distributing tacks*	*Nov. 26, 1899*	*415,726*

INVENTOR	INVENTION	DATE	PATENT
Matzeliger, J. E.	Nailing machine	Feb. 25, 1896	421,954
Matzeliger, J. E.	Tack separating mechanism	Mar. 25, 1890	423,937
Matzeliger, J. E.	Lasting machine	Mar. 20, 1883	274,207
McCoy, E.	Lubricator for steam engines	July 2, 1872	129,843
McCoy, E.	Lubricator for steam engines	Aug. 6, 1872	130,305
McCoy, E.	Steam lubricator	Jan. 20, 1874	146,697
McCoy, E.	Ironing table	May 12, 1874	150,876
McCoy, E.	Steam cylinder lubricator	Feb. 1, 1876	173,032
McCoy, E.	Steam cylinder lubricator	July 4, 1876	179,585
McCoy, E.	Lawn sprinkler design	Sept. 26, 1899	631,549
McCoy, E.	Steam dome	June 16, 1885	320,354
McCoy, E.	Lubricator attachment	Apr. 19, 1887	361,435
McCoy, E.	Lubricator for safety valves	May 24, 1887	363,529
McCoy, E.	Drip cup	Sept. 29, 1891	460,215
McCoy & Hodges	Lubricator	Dec. 24, 1889	418,139
McCree, D.	Portable fire escape	Nov. 11, 1890	440,322
Mendenhall, A.	Holder for driving reins	Nov. 28, 1899	637,811
Miles, A.	Elevator	Oct. 11, 1887	371,207
Mitchell, C. L.	Phoneterism	Jan. 1, 1884	291,071
Mitchell, J. M.	Check row corn planter	Jan. 16, 1900	641,462
Moody, W. U.	Game board design	May 11, 1897	27,046
Morehead, K.	Reel carrier	Oct. 6, 1896	568,916
Murray, G. W.	Combined furrow opener and stalk-knocker	Apr. 10, 1894	517,960
Murray, G. W.	Cultivator and marker	Apr. 10, 1894	517,961
Murray, G. W.	Planter	June 5, 1894	520,887
Murray, G. W.	Cotton chopper	June 5, 1894	520,888
Murray, G. W.	Fertilizer distributor	June 5, 1894	520,889
Murray, G. W.	Planter	June 5, 1894	520,891
Murray, G. W.	Planter and fertilizer distributor reaper	June 5, 1894	520,892
Murray, W.	Attachment for bicycles	Jan. 27, 1891	445,452
Nance, L.	Game apparatus	Dec. 1, 1891	464,035
Nash, H. H.	Life-preserving stool	Oct. 5, 1875	168,519
Newson, S.	Oil heater or cooker	May 22, 1894	520,188
Nichols & Latimer	Electric lamp (variation)	Sept. 13, 1881	247,097
Nickerson, W. J.	Mandolin and guitar attachment for pianos	June 27, 1899	627,739
O'Conner & Turner	Alarm for boilers	Aug. 25, 1896	566,612
O'Conner & Turner	Steam gage	Aug. 25, 1896	566,613
O'Conner & Turner	Alarm for coasts containing vessels	Feb. 8, 1898	598,572
Outlaw, J. W.	Horseshoes	Nov. 15, 1898	614,273
Perryman, F. R.	Caterers' tray table	Feb. 2, 1892	468,038
Perry, John Jr & Hunger, H. F.	Biochem fuel cell	Nov. 8, 1966	3,284,239

INVENTOR	INVENTION	DATE	PATENT
Peterson, H.	Attachment for lawn mowers	Apr. 30, 1889	402,189
Phelps, W. H.	Apparatus for washing vehicles	Mar. 23, 1897	579,242
Pickering, J. F.	Air ship	Feb. 20, 1900	643,975
Pickett, H.	Scaffold	June 30, 1874	152,511
Pinn, T. B.	File holder	Aug. 17, 1880	231,355
Polk, A. J.	Bicycle support	Apr. 14, 1896	558,103
Prather, Al. G. B.	Man powered glider aircraft	Feb. 6, 1973	3,715,011
Pugsley, A.	Blind stop	July 29, 1890	433,306
Purdy, W.	Device for sharpening edged tools	Oct. 27, 1896	570,337
Purdy, W.	Design for sharpening edged tools	Aug. 16, 1898	609,367
Purdy, W.	Device for sharpening edged tools	Aug. 1, 1899	630,106
Purdy & Peters	Design for spoons	Apr. 23, 1895	24,228
Purdy & Sadgwar	Folding chair	June 11, 1889	405,117
Purvis, W. B.	Bag fastener	Apr. 25, 1882	256,856
Purvis, W. B.	Hand stamp	Feb. 27, 1883	273,149
Purvis, W. B.	Fountain pen	Jan. 7, 1890	419,065
Purvis, W. B.	Electric railway (variation)	May 1, 1894	519,291
Purvis, W. B.	Magnetic car balancing device	May 21, 1895	539,542
Purvis, W. B.	Electric railway switch	Aug. 17, 1897	588,176
Queen, W.	Guard for companion ways and hatches	Aug. 18, 1891	458,131
Ray, E. P.	Chair supporting device	Feb. 21, 1899	620,078
Ray, L. P.	Dust pan	Aug. 3, 1897	587,607
Reed, J. W.	Dough kneader and roller	Sept. 23, 1884	305,474
Reynolds, H. H.	Window ventilator for railroad cars	Apr. 3, 1883	275,271
Reynolds, H. H.	Safety gate for bridges	Oct. 7, 1890	437,937
Reynolds, R. R.	Nonrefillable bottle	May 2, 1899	624,092
Rhodes, J. B.	Water closets	Dec. 19, 1899	639,290
Richardson, A. C.	Hame fastener	Mar. 14, 1882	255,022
Richardson, A. C.	Churn	Feb. 17, 1891	466,470
Richardson, A. C.	Casket-lowering device	Nov. 13, 1894	529,311
Richardson, A. C.	Insect destroyer	Feb. 28, 1899	620,363
Richardson, A. C.	Bottle	Dec. 12, 1899	638,811
Richardson, W. H.	Cotton chopper	June 1, 1886	343,140
Richardson, W. H.	Child's carriage	June 18, 1889	405,599
Richardson, W. H.	Child's carriage	June 18, 1889	405,600
Richey, C. V.	Car coupling	June 15, 1897	584,650
Richey, C. V.	Railroad switch	Aug. 3, 1897	587,657
Richey, C. V.	Railroad switch	Oct. 26, 1897	592,448
Richey, C. V.	Fire escape bracket	Dec. 28, 1897	596,427
Richey, C. V.	Combined hammock and stretcher	Dec. 13, 1898	615,907
Rickman, A. L.	Overshoe	Feb. 8, 1898	598,816

INVENTOR	INVENTION	DATE	PATENT
Ricks, J.	Horseshoe	Mar. 30, 1886	338,781
Ricks, J.	Overshoes for horses	June 6, 1899	626,245
Rillieux, N.	Sugar refiner (evaporating pan)	Dec. 10, 1846	4,879
Robinson, E. R.	Electric railway trolley	Sept. 19, 1893	505,370
Robinson, E. R.	Casting composite	Nov. 23, 1897	594,386
Robinson, J. H.	Lifesaving guards for locomotives	Mar. 14, 1899	621,143
Robinson, J. H.	Lifesaving guards for street cars	Apr. 25, 1899	623,929
Robinson, J.	Dinner pail	Feb. 1, 1887	356,852
Romain, A.	Passenger register	Apr. 23, 1889	402,035
Ross, A. L.	Runner for stops	Aug. 4, 1896	565,301
Ross, A. L.	Bag closure	June 7, 1898	605,343
Ross, A. L.	Trousers support	Nov. 28, 1899	638,068
Ross, J.	Bailing press	Sept. 5, 1899	632,539
Roster, D. N.	Feather curler	Mar. 10, 1896	556,166
Ruffin, S.	Vessels for liquids and manner of sealing	Nov. 20, 1899	737,603
Russell, L. A.	Guard attachment for beds	Aug. 13, 1895	544,381
Sampson, G. T.	Sled propeller	Feb. 17, 1885	312,388
Sampson, G. T.	Clothes drier	June 7, 1892	476,416
Scottron, S. R.	Adjustable window cornice	Feb. 17, 1880	224,732
Scottron, S. R.	Cornice	Jan. 16, 1883	270,851
Scottron, S. R.	Pole tip	Sept. 21, 1886	349,525
Scottron, S. R.	Curtain rod	Aug. 30, 1892	481,720
Scottron, S. R.	Supporting bracket	Sept. 12, 1893	505,008
Shanks, S. C.	Sleeping car berth register	July 21, 1897	587,165
Shewcraft, Frank	Letter box	NA	NA
Shorter, D. W.	Feed rack	May 17, 1887	363,089
Smith, B. & L. E. Branovich, & G. L. Freeman	Mtd. or preparing nonlaminating anisotropic Boron Nitride	Oct. 1, 1985	4,544,535
Smith, J. W.	Improvement in games	Apr. 17, 1900	647,887
Smith, J. W.	Lawn sprinkler	May 4, 1897	581,785
Smith, J. W.	Lawn sprinkler	Mar. 22, 1898	601,065
Smith, P. D.	Potato digger	Jan. 21, 1891	445,206
Smith, P. D.	Grain binder	Feb. 23, 1892	469,279
Snow & Johns	Liniment	Oct. 7, 1890	437,728
Spears, H.	Portable shield for infantry	Dec. 27, 1870	110,599
Spikes, R. B.	Combination milk bottle opener and bottle cover	June 29, 1926	1,590,557
Spikes, R. B.	Method and apparatus for obtaining average samples and temperature of tank liquids	Oct. 27, 1931	1,828,753
Spikes, R. B.	Automatic gear shift	Dec. 6, 1932	1,889,814

INVENTOR	INVENTION	DATE	PATENT
Spikes, R. B.	Transmission and shifting thereof	Nov. 28, 1933	1,936,996
Spikes, R. B.	Self-locking rack for billiard cues	ca. 1910	NA
Spikes, R. B.	Automatic shoeshine chair	ca. 1939	NA
Spikes, R. B.	Multiple barrel machine gun	ca. 1940	NA
Standard, J.	Oil stove	Oct. 29, 1889	413,689
Standard, J.	Refrigerator	July 14, 1891	455,891
Stewart, E. W.	Punching machine	May 3, 1887	362,190
Stewart, E. W.	Machine for forming vehicle seat bars	Mar. 22, 1887	373,698
Stewart, T. W.	Mop	June 13, 1893	499,402
Stewart, T. W.	Station indicator	June 20, 1893	499,895
Stewart & Johnson	Metal bending machine	Dec. 27, 1887	375,512
Sutton, E. H.	Cotton cultivator	Apr. 7, 1878	149,543
Sweeting, J. A.	Device for rolling cigarettes	Nov. 30, 1897	594,501
Sweeting, J. A.	Combined knife and scoop	June 7, 1898	605,209
Taylor, B. H.	Rotary engine	Apr. 23, 1878	202,888
Taylor, B. H.	Side valve	July 6, 1897	585,798
Temple, L.	Toggle harpoon	1848	
Thomas, S. E.	Waste trap	Oct. 16, 1883	286,746
Thomas, S. E.	Waste trap for basins, closets, etc.	Oct. 4, 1887	371,107
Thomas, S. E.	Casting	July 31, 1888	386,941
Thomas, S. E.	Pipe connection	Oct. 9, 1888	390,821
Toliver, George	Propeller for vessels	Apr. 28, 1891	451,086
Tregoning & Latimer	Globe supporter for electric lamps	Mar. 21, 1882	255,212
Walker, Peter	Machine for cleaning seed cotton	Feb. 16, 1897	577,153
Walker, Peter	Bait holder	Mar. 8, 1898	600,241
Waller, J. N.	Shoemaker's cabinet or bench	Feb. 3, 1880	244,253
Washington, Wade	Corn husking machine	Aug. 14, 1883	283,173
Watkins, Isaac	Scrubbing frame	Oct. 7, 1890	437,849
Watts, J. R.	Bracket for miners' lamp	Mar. 7, 1893	493,137
West, E. H.	Weather shield	Sept. 5, 1899	632,385
West, J. W.	Wagon	Oct. 18, 1870	108,419
White, D. L.	Extension steps for cars	Jan. 12, 1897	574,969
White, J. T.	Lemon squeezer	Dec. 8, 1896	572,849
Williams, Carter	Canopy frame	Feb. 2, 1892	468,280
Williams, J. P.	Pillow sham holder	Oct. 10, 1899	634,784
Winn, Frank	Direct acting steam engine	Dec. 4, 1888	394,047
Winters, J. R.	Fire escape ladder	May 7, 1878	203,517
Winters, J. R.	Fire escape ladder	Apr. 8, 1879	214,224
Woods, G. T.	Steam boiler furnace	June 3, 1884	299,894
Woods, G. T.	Telephone transmitter (variation)	Dec. 2, 1884	308,176

INVENTOR	INVENTION	DATE	PATENT
Woods, G. T.	*Apparatus for transmission of messages by electricity*	*Apr. 7, 1885*	*315,368*
Woods, G. T.	*Relay instrument*	*June 7, 1887*	*364,619*
Woods, G. T.	*Polarized relay*	*July 5, 1887*	*366,192*
Woods, G. T.	*Electromechanical brake*	*Aug. 16, 1887*	*368,265*
Woods, G. T.	*Telephone system and apparatus*	*Oct. 11, 1887*	*371,241*
Woods, G. T.	*Electromagnetic brake apparatus*	*Oct. 18, 1887*	*371,655*
Woods, G. T.	*Railway telegraphy*	*Nov. 15, 1887*	*373,383*
Woods, G. T.	*Induction telegraph system*	*Nov. 29, 1887*	*373,915*
Woods, G. T.	*Overhead conducting system for electric railway*	*May 29, 1888*	*383,844*
Woods, G. T.	*Electromotive railway system*	*June 26, 1888*	*385,034*
Woods, G. T.	*Tunnel construction for electric railway*	*July 17, 1888*	*386,282*
Woods, G. T.	*Galvanic battery*	*Aug. 14, 1888*	*387,839*
Woods, G. T.	*Railway telegraphy*	*Aug. 28, 1888*	*388,803*
Woods, G. T.	*Automatic safety cut-out for electric circuits*	*Jan. 1, 1889*	*395,533*
Woods, G. T.	*Automatic safety cut-out for electric circuits*	*Oct. 14, 1889*	*438,590*
Woods, G. T.	*Electric railway system*	*Nov. 10, 1891*	*463,020*
Woods, G. T.	*Electric railway supply system*	*Oct. 31, 1893*	*507,606*
Woods, G. T.	*Electric railway conduit*	*Nov. 21, 1893*	*509,065*
Woods, G. T.	*System of electrical distribution*	*Oct. 13, 1896*	*569,443*
Woods, G. T.	*Amusement apparatus*	*Dec. 19, 1899*	*639,692*
Wormley, James	*Lifesaving apparatus*	*May 24, 1881*	*242,091*

bibliography

Adams, Russell L. *Great Negroes, Past and Present*, rev. ed. Chicago: Afro-Am Publishing Co., Inc., 1984.

Balch, S. W. *Cosmopolitan Magazine*, vol. 18 (April 1895): 761–62.

Barrows, Samuel J. "What the Southern Negro Is Doing for Himself." *Atlantic Monthly*, vol. 57 (June 1891): 810–15.

Butcher, Margaret Just. *The Negro in American Culture*. New York: New American Library, 1971.

"Celebrating America's Black Inventors: The Real McCoy." *Inventor's Digest*, November/December 1989: 6–7, 18.

Dannett, Sylvia G. L. *Profiles of Negro Womanhood*. Yonkers, N.Y.: Educational Heritage, Inc.

Editors of *American Heritage. American Manners and Morals*. New York: American Heritage Publishing Co., 1969.

Frazier, E. Franklin. *The Negro Family in the United States*. Chicago: University of Chicago Press, 1939.

Hayden, Robert. *Seven Black American Scientists*. New York: Addison-Wesley, 1970.

Hayes, Joanne M. "Famous People and Their 'Not-so-Famous' Inventions." *Inventor's Digest,* September/ October 1989: 8–9.

Hughes, Langston, and Milton Meltzer. *A Pictorial History of the Negro in America,* 3rd rev. ed. New York: Crown Publishing, 1970.

Jackson, Florence. *The Black Man in America: 1791– 1861.* New York: Franklin Watts, 1971.

————. *The Black Man in America: 1877–1905.* New York: Franklin Watts, 1973.

Katz, William L. *Eyewitness: The Negro in American History.* New York: Pitman Publishing Corp., 1967.

Morris, Saurian. *A Sketch of the Life of Benjamin Banneker: Own Notes Taken in 1836.* Baltimore, MD: Maryland Historical Society, 1854.

Ploski, Harry A., and James Williams, eds. *The Negro Almanac: A Reference Work on the African American.* Detroit: Gale Research, Inc., 1989.

The Smithsonian Book of Invention. Washington, D.C.: Smithsonian Exposition Books, Smithsonian Institution, 1978.

index